JONATHAN FIRTH

Creative Thinking

Contents

Introduction

"It's still magic even if you know how it's done" - Terry Pratchett, novelist.[1]

Creativity is the process of making something new that is useful to us in some way. Some creative works will be of great significance, such as literary work that could impact on society as a whole, or a musical composition or scientific theory that is truly original. Others will be smaller in scale – perhaps a neat solution to a problem at home or in the workplace. Either way, a set of psychological processes is involved, drawing on our memory and our skills, and combining ideas in new ways.

Our minds naturally tend towards creative and imaginative thinking, and humans' ability to come up with creative solutions to problems may well have been essential to the survival of our species in previous generations[2]. For example, our early ancestors, living in small tribes on the equatorial savannah or in rocky coastal caves, were faced with a complex environment and numerous threats, from predators to the risk of starvation. Those who were able to come up with new solutions to these problems – weapons for self-defence, food preservation, and so on – put themselves at a survival advantage.

Indeed, almost everything around us – from houses to cars to mobile phones to the art of writing – is the product of creative thinking by people who have gone before us. And this process hasn't stopped – new ideas are developed every day.

Creativity in society

It can be argued that creativity is as fundamentally important to our lives education as literacy and numeracy. Indeed, perhaps it is even more fundamental than either of those basic skills. In his book, '*Out of our minds*', TED talk speaker and British author Ken Robinson said, "If all you had was academic ability, you wouldn't have been able to get out of bed this morning. In fact, there wouldn't have been a bad to get out of. No one could have made one"[3].

Creative problem solving is also much older than formal academic education. Human creativity was applied to practical problems such as hunting or building long before the existence of schools. Early societies drew on creativity for pleasure, too – there was already music, oral storytelling, painting and sculpture before writing was developed in around 4th millennium BC, and it is likely that these creative arts were of major significance to early societies.

Today, culture has advanced to the extent that people have more time (or the potential for more time) to spend on creative pursuits than they once did, in part because humankind has largely found technical solutions to many of the great problems that made life so precarious in the past. As tasks such as agriculture, manufacturing and driving become partly or entirely automated, people will need to find new roles, with the majority of the laborious work which once occupied our time no longer a necessity [4]. This frees people up to consider what gives them a sense of value and purpose. In the world of work, too, people are increasingly questioning what they want to do and sometimes changing careers several times across their working lives, in contrast to the past expectation that a career would last a lifetime.

As humanity progresses further into the 21st century, the question for most people in the world is not just how to survive, but how to make life worth living. Creative pursuits are life-affirming and engaging – they are the things that help us rise above the daily grind.

Your Creativity

For you as an individual, creativity comes in many forms. There are certain tasks that society has tended to associate with creativity – making works of art, creative writing, composing songs, and so on. However, these reflect just a few of the ways that people can think creatively. Creative processes can be of benefit to many other areas of life, from the development of good ideas to the honing of original and high-quality work. Some major possibilities include:

- Coming up with new ideas at in your job
- Writing non-fiction reports, books or guides
- Thinking of better ways to run a household
- Developing scientific research and theories
- Developing a successful product or business strategy

We also create in much more practical and everyday ways – thinking of a new way to organise your belongings, or a good idea for how to spend your weekend that incorporates several of your interests at once.

Regardless of the pursuit or context involved, creative though requires applying your existing knowledge in new ways, and this book will guide you through the process.

Using the book

This book is a simple, ready-to-use set of techniques, each based on the cognitive psychology of thinking and learning. It is not an abstract, theoretical work – the techniques are designed to be ready for you to use immediately to boost the effectiveness and the quality of your creative pursuits, to increase the number of good ideas you have, and to put them into action so that you are more successfully productive.

The strategies described in the coming chapters can help you with a major creative endeavour such completing a novel that you've got on the back burner, but can also help you be more creative and successful in your career, and to come up with diverse and brilliant ideas for hobbies and projects.

All the strategies are practical rather than theoretical, but they are deeply rooted in theories and research evidence which have been studied systematically for many decades. All of the research studies that back up each strategy are listed at the end of the book, and I would encourage anyone with an interest in the psychology of creativity to delve into some of these as further reading.

The book is divided into two main sections. The first, "Thoughts and Ideas", focuses on the knowledge, thinking and creative transfer needed to develop and use ideas in a creative way. After all, we need to have ideas if we are to produce anything novel. The second, "Craft and Habits", refers more to the working procedures which lead to prolific and high-quality creative output. It's no use having lots of ideas if you don't develop them and bring them to fruition as part of a successful project.

The techniques are set out in what seemed to be a logical order, but they could just as easily be read in any order that takes your interest. As will be discussed later, creativity is not only about the creation of entirely new ideas, but also involves reflecting on existing ideas and tools, and using these in new and unfamiliar ways instead of following an obvious path or script (more on scripts later!).

Finally, it's important to note that these ideas are not one-off quick fixes. You can't develop creativity in a single afternoon; it's a gradual and sometimes lifelong process of developing habits and strategies. However, at its base is a set of behaviours and skills which you can start to hone right now, allowing you to begin to produce more exciting, clever and satisfying ideas and outcomes. It may help if you have a particular project in mind as you work through this book, but you can return to it again and again as you tackle new projects, writings or art.

Good luck with all of your creative endeavours!

I

THOUGHTS AND IDEAS

This part of the book looks at the processes involved in coming up with successful creative ideas, from the initial process of making original connections to generating fully formed ideas, drawing on both your own knowledge and on other people around you. It also looks at the habits of mind needed for creativity, including focus, effective use of breaks and rest, and achieving the 'flow' state.

Strategy 1: Generating Ideas

"My problematic ideas are my favourite ones. Because they feel the most genuine."
    Ayishat Akanbi, stylist.[5]

I n any creative project, from writing a novel to planning your next world tour, there is always some kind of starting point: an idea, or perhaps a set of several ideas from which you need to select the best ones. So, where do these ideas come from, and what can you do in order to have more of the kind of ideas you need?

The first point to make is that ideas don't come from nowhere. Contrary to the beliefs of the Ancient Greeks – who thought that creative inspiration came from demi-gods known as *Muses* – we now know that ideas come from the brain, and in particular from your memory (although interestingly, Greek creation myths also state that the Muses were the children of Mnemosyne, the goddess of memory).

Using your memory doesn't mean that you are simply re-calling old ideas. Instead, it is a recognition that ideas often involve making new connections among things you already know. In order to do this, you need to develop effective thinking strategies for recalling and recombining the material which you have stored in your long-term memory throughout your life so far.

There are a number of techniques which can help, but one of the oldest and most successful is *brainstorming.* This means coming up with a list of as many thoughts as possible in a non-critical context, not judging or rejecting but purely adding whatever comes to mind. Most of these will not be useful ideas in themselves, but will provide the raw material that can then be analysed and combined, changed, used, or simply rejected.

Although the term brainstorming may have negative connotations (perhaps it sounds a bit like a form of management speak), it actually fits well with what psychologists know about how the mind works. It links to one of the most-used psychometric tests of creativity, devised in the mid-20[th]Century by psychologist Joy Paul Guilford – the task where a person is asked to think of as many uses as possible for a simple object such as a paperclip or a brick.

Guilford was dissatisfied by attempts to characterise human thinking in terms of a single number – the IQ score. He felt that human mental abilities were more complex, composed of several processes. *Divergent thinking*, the ability to come up with multiple solutions, was one such ability [6].

Guilford's model of intelligence is largely forgotten today, but the creativity test is still used in many research studies as part of what is known as the *alternative uses test*, which can be used either to test how many ideas someone has (how many uses for each item) or how original they are (by comparing them to a bank of previous answers). An interesting finding among such studies is that although measured intelligence levels have gradually risen among the school population, scores on creativity have been falling. While it's not entirely clear why that's the case, it's possible that standardised tests with their emphasis on intensive practice to get the 'right answer' fail to develop the skills involved in thinking broadly and coming up with new and unexpected ideas.

A key element of brainstorming is to focus on quantity over quality, maintaining a non-critical approach and keeping all ideas in play at first, however stupid or irrelevant they might seem. A later review stage is then used to discard the less promising ones, but – hopefully – find one or two rough diamonds that can then be worked upon. This can mean keeping all notes, and reviewing them at a later point.

Despite the difficulty of researching this technique, it has been shown to be an effective way of generating ideas, especially if people have been trained in how to use it[7]. Research by Paul Paulus and colleagues at the University of Texas has found that it helps to initially generate categories ('what types of thing am I going to think of?'), and then use these categories one at a time as prompts for several follow-up brainstorming sessions [8]. For example, a novelist could begin by thinking about the kinds of things they want to know about a new character (e.g. things that they own, their appearance, their habits...) and then work through these one at a time as brainstorm prompts, spending a few minutes on each one.

The key to successful brainstorming is to be non-critical, throwing many ideas into the mix and letting one thought lead to the next, as well as getting into a relaxed but focused frame of mind. In this sense, it is rather similar to the technique Sigmund Freud developed for therapy, whereby patients would let one idea lead to the next in a process of 'free association' [9]. Freud believed that this allowed subconscious thoughts and desires to be revealed; creativity, too, is often associated with the subconscious (see also **Strategy 8**). It is important not to get distracted from the process (or stop altogether) after generating one or two exciting ideas, but instead to note each one down, and continue trying to think of more.

How long should we brainstorm for? The type of memory involved in forming associations can be slow; it can therefore take a while for things to be remembered or useful links to be made. From this point of view, it would be well worth taking at least 20 minutes on a single brainstorming session. Interestingly, this is also around about the daily length of time which some writers say we should spend on freewriting – see **Strategy 8**. More importantly, don't stop or move on immediately, even if you feel that you are running out of good ideas. This is important, because the research of Paul Paulus's team has shown that the best ideas tend to be produced later in a session. It isn't inherently a bad thing if you feel stuck, or that many your ideas are poor and will be discarded. Additionally, taking breaks needn't always be a problem – forming mental associations can depend on input from the outside world, so it may be more productive to do several short sessions rather than one long one. The later sessions will need to be reasonably long, too.

Although brainstorming tends to be viewed as the starting point of a project, a similar principle can be applied throughout the creative process – new ideas are first generated, and then later evaluated, and (where appropriate) integrated into the creative work. Author Fay Weldon says that a writer needs two personalities: the creator of first drafts who is sloppy, emotional and impetuous, and the later editor who is argumentative, cautious and rational[10]. Connecting the previous points, then, a series of 20-minute brainstorming sessions could be worked in at several stages throughout a project, allowing previous thoughts and newly learned information or feedback to be productively synthesised.

Brainstorming in groups can sometimes help, and may be highly appropriate for some contexts such as a shared research project or working on an album as part of a band. In some cases, though – and for some personalities – it can harm performance and decrease the quality of ideas due to the pressures and anxiety linked with a group setting. In short, the feeling of being judged is not conducive to the flow of ideas. One way around this could be to brainstorm individually first, then discuss the better ideas with one or more trusted individuals, followed by further individual brainstorming. Many creative artists have a small group of friends or colleagues who look over early versions of their work before these are ready to be shared more publicly, and this can be a reciprocal arrangement.

Key tips:

- Set aside 15-20 minute blocks of time at the start of your creative process, and periodically during each project.
- Think of a list of categories, then brainstorm on these one by one. Try to come up uncritically with ideas – write down everything, no matter how stupid or useless it seems at first.
- If you find writing the ideas down distracting, try typing or voice recording yourself – voice recorder apps can automatically transcribe what you say.
- Setting up a system where you file your brainstormed ideas. Return to these periodically, and use the best ones as stimuli for further brainstorming.

Strategy 2: Developing Expert Skill

"It took me thirty years to do that masterpiece in thirty seconds."
Pablo Picasso, visual artist.[11]

C reativity can be hard work. It's not a coincidence that the most culturally significant creative ideas come from individuals who have years of experience, and have developed a high level of skill and expert knowledge in their field. For example, Adam Smith was 53 years old when he wrote his classic work of economic politics, *The Wealth of Nations*, and Karl Marx worked on *Das Kapital* for 26 years, dying before it was complete.

Even in cases where great discoveries appear to be very rapid, there is often more to the story. For example, Marie Curie gained a degree in 1894, discovered that uranium emits radiation in 1896, and in 1898 she published work that led to her Nobel Prize. However, Curie had from 1890 studied and taught at the "floating university", a secretive institution which allowed women to study at degree level when this was still not allowed officially in France or in her native Warsaw. Prior to this, Curie had already been steeped in science and scholarship from a young age; her father taught mathematics and physics, and when she graduated from school she gained the gold medal for her year. She then engaged in tutoring and self-study throughout the late 1880s, was known as an avid reader, and fanatically diligent researcher[12]. None of this reduces the value of what Curie produced, but it does show that brilliant ideas tend to be preceded by an in-depth learning process, rather than being random strokes of genius.

The good news is that you don't need to be an expert in everything, and can be selective within a particular field or creative pursuit. However, the more you learn about the subject in question, the better. For most people who are not at the cutting edge of science, their subject matter may be relatively restricted and fall within everyday general knowledge. You don't need to be an expert on literary criticism to write a good short story, for example, but you do need to know a lot about the subject matter of the story. Immerse yourself in this knowledge, learning about all the details you can, however trivial. If there are locations involved, walk around these as possible, taking notes or photographs. Test yourself on all of this a few days later – because forgetting is rapid, and knowledge relies on long-term engagement with the material. This is true even with regard to features that don't seem important at first glance, as memory relies on complex interlinked associations – details that you don't actually use may help to trigger ideas and guide your thinking.

If you are already at the cutting edge of your area of interest, for example in science, business, technology or musical composition, you already have a lot of the expert knowledge that you need. Great! It remains important for you to develop, consolidate and refine that knowledge, ensuring that it comes easily to mind.

Ideas are not going to spark off each other in your notebooks – the knowledge has to be in your brain. How well can you remember the details of your last project, or the previous story or paper that you wrote? Do you know it *by heart*? Most of us know only a few lines or quotes that well. That's entirely normal, but experts can bring key details to mind immediately. So revisit previous work regularly.

It might seem that this technique is advocating cluttering the brain with useless information, but far from it. For one thing, it's difficult to say in advance what will be useful and what won't. Sometimes, ideas come from the strangest set of associations. Secondly, your brain cannot get full – human long-term memory has no known limit. This is because new learning doesn't involve creating new storage in the brain, but depends on making new connections and strengthening existing connections between brain cells – processes that can happen indefinitely.

Robert Bjork, a psychologist at the University of California and an expert on real-world applications of memory, believes that forgetting is of less importance than accessibility. In other words, once something has been well learned once it doesn't disappear, but instead just gets harder to access with the passage of time. This can happen to any memory, unless accessed regularly [13]. The more you keep using information, especially using it *actively* in varied contexts with gaps of time in between, the better. In this sense, storage of information in the brain is nothing like computer storage (to which it is often compared) – recall of what you have learned depends mainly on how and when you use the information.

Another way that our memory abilities differ from a computer is that adding new knowledge makes it *easier* to access and use information. Just ask anyone who has learned several languages – they will tell you that the later ones were easier to learn than the first. The brain doesn't get full, and it actually works faster for having more knowledge.

Developing knowledge is not a passive activity. Educational-ists have known for years that active learning is more effective than passive re-reading or listening (not that those are entirely ineffective, but they are only a starting point). This is especially important in the field of creativity, because when engaged in brainstorming or other activities relating to creative thinking, it's important to be able to think of things almost effortlessly. To use the psychological terms, the knowledge has to become so familiar that it is almost *automatic* for you to retrieve it. The key message from this technique is to keep using all of the information that is relevant to your creative pursuits – summarise it, retrieve it, try it in different places, talk about it. If you do this for long enough, it will become second nature, and you will have developed deep, flexible knowledge which will help new ideas come easily to mind.

Key tips:

- Test yourself and re-use information and skills after a delay, because intensive learning leads to a lot of forgetting.
- Use information out of the context in which you learned it. For example, if you regularly read in your own home, try changing to a waiting room, football stadium, graveyard...
- Actively use information – for example, by telling a friend about it – rather than re-reading it.

Strategy 3: Looking for Connections

"Creativity involves cognitive processes that transform one's understanding of, or relationship to, the world."
  Liane Gabora, researcher.[14]

Where do creative people get their ideas from? One possible answer to this is that they are highly observant, constantly noticing things in their surroundings, people watching, and storing good ideas for future use. But it's also important to make the most of these experiences – and sometimes this involves connecting several different ideas into something new.

Robert Sternberg, former president of the American Psychological Association, created a 'triarchic' theory of intelligence, which presented creativity as one of the three main aspects of intelligent thought. Like Guilford (see **Strategy 1**), he felt that theories of intelligence and IQ were too narrow. The triarchic theory aimed to show that intelligence is not just about what happens in your head, but also how you react to situations in the real world. As the name suggests, there are three strands to it, called 'subtheories' – the first of which relates mainly to the traditional view of intelligence – reasoning, knowledge acquisition, problem solving and so forth. The other two emphasise more creative thinking – an 'experiential' subtheory about how we use learned information to find new solutions, and a 'contextual' subtheory, about how people adapt to problems in the real world [15].

Together with his colleague Todd Lubart, Sternberg defined an act as creative if it involves making something new or finding an original re-combination of existing elements, provided that the end result is useful in some way [16]. Something could be new but not useful, and therefore not considered creative – any random combination of words or musical notes fits this description. Likewise, something could be useful but not new (although it might be new to you).

This definition helps by placing our focus on new combinations of existing ideas, making novel mental connections. Following on from the previous strategy, creative ideas don't come from nowhere, but involve well-understood and easily remembered elements being put together in novel ways – like building something out of reused Lego bricks. This is why it's so important to have a base of factual knowledge and skills in your field, and it's what separates mature creative work from the creative play seen among children.

This facet of creativity was recognised by enlightenment philosophers. For example, the great French writer Voltaire described originality as being "*nothing but judicious imitation*". This is more than just a comic observation – although Voltaire was himself startlingly original, he highlights the idea that new work is often largely elements from older ones, polished up and put into a new framework. Most novels, articles, projects or artworks don't produce something that has never been done before, but they take already recognisable characters, actions and plot-lines and weave them together in a way that is new and exciting. Indeed, something has to be at least recognisable to be considered a part of the art form or genre at all.

The same can apply to some of the great new ideas of science. In the 1800s, Charles Darwin took three key ideas – the new geological theory of timescales devised by Hutton and others, Malthus's economic observations on population growth and his own observations of species variation – and combined them into his principles of evolution via natural selection [17].

What this tells us is that it's not always the building blocks themselves that are important, but the skill of noticing connections, looking at things from new angles, and toying with new combinations. This kind of originality depends on thinking strategies and habits of thought. When people think, there is the tendency to do things in traditional, tried-and-tested ways. Metaphorically, it's like following a path through the long grass simply because it is natural to put one foot in front of another where it's easier to do so. By following the well-trodden path, we will find ourselves doing things the same way they have been done before – that is to say, lacking originality in our work. How, then, do we break away from repetition of known and recognisable patterns and do something unique, finding new ways of arranging what we already know?

As mentioned above, psychologists know that thinking draws heavily on memory, and that our knowledge is not stored as separate facts, but is instead based on complex interconnections. The more a particular memory or association is accessed, the easier it is to access in the future – while competing memories become harder to retrieve. This was demonstrated in a clever experiment led by Michael Anderson of the University of Cambridge. The researchers presented pairs of words to participants such as FRUIT-ORANGE, and then tested them with one of the pair (e.g. FRUIT-?). Not only did people better remember the partner word ('orange', in this example), they were worse at remembering other alternatives than a control group. So, if told that they needed to think of another type of fruit, they took longer than someone who hadn't studied the pair of words [18].

Our brains are probably set up to find these regular connections and act on them, as throughout our evolution, working out what goes with what will have been an essential aspect of survival to our ancestors – this forest is full of fruit trees, for example, while the other one is full of predators. However, originality must involve breaking away from obvious and well-learned responses.

One approach is to seek out and value serendipity – developing a habit of looking at the bizarre or flawed and analysing it for potential. There are many examples of artists who have either deliberately looked for new and unusual combinations of elements/ideas in their work or who have benefited from this by accident. The Dadaist school of poetry took it to an extreme by cutting up newspaper articles, and then pulling out words one by one to form an accidental, surreal form of poem. Many inventions and scientific developments are also said to have been inspired by accidents, although they are of course based on a deep professional expertise that allowed their creators to recognise the potential of those accidents. On a more regular basis, everyday conversations and life events can spark creative ideas that provide the raw material for works of fiction.

To force some of these unconventional connections to occur, it can be useful to mix up the order of prompts and events, putting things side by side that are not usually seen as being connected. When researching or studying prior work in your field, this could involve varying the order of items, rather than working through an entire artist's back catalogue or sticking to a particular genre. Rather than categorising your books by genre, try selecting a random assortment and trying to think of similarities and differences between them. The same applies to other media such as visual art and music.

Existing patterns can be useful when you are new to an area and first developing your expertise (see **Strategy 2**), as they generally help you to understand how things work. For example, any new author could benefit from recognising that story structure includes certain universal elements. But there also comes a point in the creative process where we start to play with these basic elements. In other words, we have a firm enough grasp of the basics to begin to experiment, and see what effect this will have.

Researchers know that experts think and remember in different ways from novices. They access information more quickly and are better at filtering out non-essential details and seeing the big picture [19]. They also ask more questions [20] – a counterintuitive finding, as it might be assumed that it would be novices who would ask more, because of their lower levels of knowledge. Experts ask questions because they focus on things that seem inconsistent or don't fit with their prior expectations. All of this means that it will be easier to make the "ah-ha!" connections once you have already established at least the beginnings of expertise in your area.

A lot of learning and thinking involves categorising things into groups, and making new distinctions between groups as we notice subtle differences. According to psychologist Eleanor Rosch, categories don't exist in the world, but are created in the mind to serve a particular purpose – they make the world simpler to understand, so that it's easier to engage in everyday thinking[21]. As such, children categorise the world in simpler ways than adults (e.g. they may refer to 'bugs' while an adult knows there are various type of insect). Experts categorise into even finer sub-categories (an entomologist, for example, knows that there are hundreds of types of beetle).

Research into inductive learning – that is, learning via examples – has found that we are better at learning about categories when we see examples in a way that is mixed up or interleaved. For example, researchers Sean Kang and Luke Eglington presented learners with examples of chemical molecules of different types, showing contrasting molecular structure types mixed together. Compared to a group who were shown multiple examples of the same type, their later ability to correctly identify previously unseen examples was better[22]. Perhaps the accidental benefits of mixing as a way of comparing and prompting connections is one reason why artists and scientists stereotypically have messy desks and studies – helping to stimulate unusual new ideas.

A mind map (or 'concept map') is a systematic tool that can be used to encourage new associations. It is a method of note taking which links words and ideas in a cluster or spider-shaped diagram, with a central idea as its hub. It is sometimes recommended as an aid to memory, but drawing these maps tends to be time consuming, making it somewhat inefficient compared to other ways of taking notes or revising facts[23]. However, the non-linear form of a mind map can be very helpful for noticing the structure of a set of ideas, and for triggering non-obvious connections in your mind, possibilities that might have been quickly discarded if they weren't down on paper.

Other types of note taking could also benefit from being freer in form. While it is of course important that you can find information in your notes, there is a cost of being too rigid and structured – it can limit the ease with which the mind spots interesting new connections. Categorising too strictly can be problematic, as it makes it harder to connect distant concepts. One way to balance the need for order (so you can find specific sets of notes quickly) with the potential benefits of accidental new connections is to label or date everything at the top of a page, rather than having them appear sequentially in a notebook. Using several notebooks or multiple sheets of loose leaf paper could help you to accidentally spot and think about an older set of ideas and how these might inform or fit in with what you are working on right now.

A *bullet journal* is another great way of simultaneously organising your notes and allowing a freer form, with multiple connections – it essentially functions as a diary, journal and to-do list in one. It involves a contents page or index that is constantly updated, and which is used to structure the other sections.

Older notes and note books are also worth revisiting periodically, as there may be half-developed ideas lurking which suddenly spark an idea that you missed at the time (see **Strategy 10**). There are also many apps such as Evernote that allow you to scan notes and store them in a way that is easily accessible and searchable, although it's important to question whether the format allows you to review old notes sufficiently easily. An advantage of paper or printed formats is that it's easier to gather old sheets, prompts or half-finished works in a form that is easily reviewed. Ideally, it should also be possible for such notes to be re-ordered (having them on separate sheets or index cards, for example). Occasionally, try leafing through such sources without a particular purpose in mind – this may spark new connections more effectively than searching for particular content. This kind of work (and don't forget that generating ideas really is work!) is best done late at night or first thing in the morning **(see Strategy 9)**, not during the time when you are normally at your most productive (otherwise it could easily become a form of procrastination).

Taking the previous idea one step further, you could establish a specific set of prompts on slips of paper or index cards – words, quotes, musical phrases, pictures, characters, or whatever is appropriate to your field, and the more the better. These could be from your own work, from other people's, or a mixture. When you have some free time, shuffle them like a deck of cards, and pick several at random. Try to come up with an idea that incorporates as many as possible of the prompts. Using a timer, brainstorm or mind map on this selection. Children enjoy such tasks as they have game-like elements, and it could be a fun and motivating way to start a creative session. If you are lucky, you will come up with some fascinating new connections, and if not, at least it will get you started in an enjoyable way and prepare the mind for creative thinking by activating memories of several things that inspire you.

There are also external ways of finding suitable prompts. Flicking through books of photographs or ideas – even if they are unrelated to your field – can stimulate interesting connections. Some fields have ready-made examples, such as the creative writer prompts available in books or via daily emails. An alternative for other creative fields is the fascinating "Oblique Strategies" created by musician Brian Eno together with Peter Schmidt. These are a set of cards in a box, which aim to "*break creative deadlock*" by presenting new ways of looking at a problem[24]. In essence, they help to provide a different perspective, or inject an element of randomisation and chaos that can prevent you from becoming stuck on a particular thought or process (see also **Strategy 17**).

Mixing up your thinking and making more varied connections also help with tackling a related issue – the difficulty in linking information or skills to new contexts. Psychologists and educators refer to this ability as *transfer*, and it is fundamentally creative – successful transfer involves making links between familiar ideas and new situations. We often practice and hone our skills in a single location and context, but the more ideas are connected to a specific setting, the harder it gets to use them more broadly. Linking your creative work to different places and occasions will be very helpful to future transfer of your skills, boosting your ability to make new and more original connections in the future.

Key tips:

- Remember that creativity is less about finding 'the great idea' and more about combining existing elements in new ways.
- Find strategies for putting things together in unusual or unexpected orders in a way that works in your creative field.
- Begin creative sessions with a fun task, combining randomly selected prompts. Build up a set of these prompts over time. These can help you to get in the right frame of mind, and may help to trigger a unique new association that proves valuable, and to transfer your ideas to unfamiliar settings in the future.

Strategy 4: Flow, and the Role of Attention

"The whole project went very fast. It all seemed absolutely brand new."
   Brice Marden, visual artist.[25]

In the discussion about generating ideas, above (see **Strategy 1**), it was noted that the best ideas from brainstorming often come later in a session. This may be because it takes time to get into the right emotional frame of mind, developing sufficient focus on the material at hand but also getting relaxed enough to produce new ideas uncritically without feeling anxious or embarrassed.

The state of being both relaxed and focused is sometimes described as a *flow* state, and appears to play a central role in successful creativity. Flow can be defined as a combination of high focus and absorption during a task. It occurs when we are challenged, but our skill level is sufficient to meet the challenge. In such a state, people tend to feel alert, motivated and happy, though not necessarily outwardly cheerful.

The flow theory was developed by Hungarian psychologist Mihaly Csíkszentmihályi during his time at the University of

Chicago, as he attempted to explain why some people feel more absorbed and content in situations such as work and sport. It didn't seem to be entirely down to ability, but he had a hunch that the level of challenge needed to be right for the individual – not to difficult, but not too easy, either.

Time seems to pass quickly when we are in the flow state, and external distractions are barely noticed. A couple of hours may pass and seem like only a fraction of that time. Take a minute to think of an activity when you have felt like this. What characteristics does that activity have? Usually, a flow state only occurs when you enjoy the task; it must be complex enough that completing it is not routine, and can't be done with half of your attention (this applies to all creative tasks!). It's also critical that you have sufficient competence in the task that you can act without needing to repeatedly stop and check what to do or how to do it.

Flow is not the same as being *relaxed*, and certainly doesn't mean that your mind is wandering off – daydreaming while driving or cleaning does not indicate a flow state. Rather, it involves becoming totally absorbed in and focused on the task itself. We have probably all experienced this when reading a great novel, or when playing games as a child. The experience of asking, 'is it that time already?' is an indication that we have been experiencing flow. This steady focus tends to make tasks more enjoyable and increase success, while achieving a flow state in the workplace is associated with higher job satisfaction [26]

For most people, flow is not easily achieved in new creative endeavours, because such tasks are very difficult. When some- one first starts to draw or paint, for example, they make many mistakes, and spend a lot of time thinking about the details of technique and materials. It is similar in other fields – a new researcher or beginner novelist may find that they are struggling with and getting frustrated with technical details, an issue which will harm their ability to become absorbed in the creative process itself. This, then, connects to **Strategy 2** – the better your skill and expert knowledge, the more easily you will achieve a flow state.

For the creative individual to achieve flow when engaged in the development of a new task or project, too much of a focus on how the end product will be received by an audience or by critics is likely to be counterproductive. In order to avoid worrying about outcomes or experiencing the 'fear of the blank page', it can be necessary to eschew thinking about the end product at all. Instead, the aim is to become immersed in the task. Even conscious attention on the future steps in a project could be harmful, as it leads to directing attention away from the creative task. Focusing on a specific short-term goal can help to boost flow in such situations.

It may also help to forget about the quality of the end result, and create as if you are just doing it for fun. This doesn't mean that self-criticism is a bad thing – over the longer term it may be helpfully interspersed with moments of pure absorption. But as with brainstorming, too much 'big picture' thinking can be a distraction – the time for overall evaluation of your work or editing can come later.

It is also vital to avoid using up attention on distracting minor tasks. The reason that it is so important to clear distractions is that our attention has a limited capacity. One way to think about attention is to view it like a cake that can be divided up into slices – but slicing off parts for another task makes the main slice smaller, and therefore you will do your main creative task more poorly if distracted. It can therefore be seen as a resource that is limited at any given time. Attention will be greatly affected if we try to multitask, and is also reduced by tiredness or stress.

Your mind also tends to focus a fraction of its attention on future tasks that you know you have to do, such as putting the dinner on, going to a meeting or picking the kids up from school. Researchers call this *prospective memory* – memory for things that you need to do in the future. This kind of mental load is unhelpful to achieving a flow state, and likewise flow can lead to you forgetting about other duties. You have probably had the experience at some point of missing an appointment because you became absorbed in something more enjoyable and lost track of time. From a creativity point of view, this is a good thing. The lack of such responsibilities may be one reason that children can apparently get into a flow state more easily (for example during play) than is the case for their parents.

It is therefore important, where possible, to clear external distractions in order to increase the chances of achieving a flow state. This can include identifying the time of day when it is easiest for you to work without distractions, and without obligations that are likely to play on your mind. You may find that it's easier to get caught up in a novel in the evening after work, or to progress with a coding project after the kids have been taken to school and you know that you have a few hours before anything else urgent needs to be done.

One simple technique is to set alarms for any responsibilities that you must achieve later in the day, and that you might otherwise forget, so that they are cleared from your immediate conscious attention span. Find a place where you are comfortable working, with phone off, and internet off if necessary. Better still, put your phone away entirely; research in the workplace has found that the rejuvenating effect of a break is undermined if the break is spent on your phone[27].

Of course, some people have very busy and somewhat chaotic lives. It may be very difficult indeed to find a chunk of time when you can forget about everything else. Perhaps it will be possible in some cases to tinker with your schedule – making use of the early morning before others are up, the late evening, or the commute, for example. But if necessary, good creative work can be achieved in shorter bursts. You don't need to achieve a flow state all of the time – but if it happens at least occasionally, it suggests that you are getting close to the ideal balance of task difficulty and skill.

It's worth briefly mentioning the role of *working memory* and multi-tasking, here. Working memory is a set of psychological functions involved in thinking about and doing tasks in the here-and-now. It depends upon attention (which can be seen as the fuel of working memory), and has several components including verbal and visual processing, and the ability to combine sets of events into a coherent experience[28].

What is clear, however, is that (like attention) working memory is very limited. Because of these limitations, it's much harder to do two things at a time, especially if these things are unrelated, and almost impossible to sustain such multi-tasking over longer period of time. As per the stereotype, women do appear to be slightly better at multi-tasking than men[29], but everyone gets worse if they try to do more than one task at a time.

Key tips:

- The absorption known as 'flow' occcurs when both ability and challenge are at a high level. Bear in mind that tasks which are too simple will lead to unhelpful mind wandering.
- In order to achieve the flow state, focus on a single goal at a time.
- Allocate yourself a generous amount of time with no distractions, ensuring that you are comfortable at the start. Don't schedule in phone calls or have an additional 'to do' list at the back of your mind. Instead, take your creative work seriously, and clear a block of time in your schedule.

Strategy 5: Drawing on Other People

"It's not like you see songs approaching and invite them in. You want to say something about strange things that you have seen".
   Bob Dylan, musician and visual artist.[30]

For all that the previous strategies have focused on your own individual thoughts, emotions and memories, creativity does not tend to be entirely a solo endeavour. Indeed, there's not much that's truly original, and all of the great artists, composers and writers have influences that have shaped their work. Bob Dylan developed the work of Woodie Guthrie. Emile Zola's novels were inspired by the scientific work of Claude Bernard, and Zola's work in turn influenced the development of the naturalistic novel in Brazil. Shakespeare leant heavily on works of history such as Plutarch's *Parallel Lives* as he developed his masterpieces (and some of Shakespeare's plays such as *Titus Andronicus* are thought to have been collaborations).

Experiencing the work of others can be highly motivational. Some creatives set themselves up for the day's work by enjoying work that inspires them; in his book *On Writing*, Steven King describes his habit of listening to music at the start of a writing session, while some crossword setters solve a few simple puzzles themselves in order to get their mind in the right place for creating their own[31]. Reading a great novel, hearing a song, re-reading a favourite research paper... It is a good idea to take as many opportunities as you can to engage with the creative work of others. And you can choose to draw on whatever is relevant and is likely to make you feel relaxed and inspired. As well as boosting mood and focusing your attention, this preparatory work can also lead to noticing ideas and gaps in knowledge that you can take forward into the day's work.

New artists may fear that drawing on others will lead to pro-ducing work that is derivative, but it is important to recognise the need to build on ideas that have gone before – this helps creativity, rather than harming it. One technique to avoid being overwhelmed by the quality of work we admire is to develop a more critical or evaluative mindset – what didn't they do well? Why might someone dislike this? Can you identify a specific aspect of the work that you could take on and develop? In the case of an artist or scientist who is no longer with us, what problem might they work on if they were still alive today? If the work of your favourite creative artists or scientists just seems to be too perfect for you to criticise, why not look instead at the work that inspired them, for example the North African art or historical events that inspired Picasso? Digging back into the historical record can help you understand the context of seminal works, and see what issues they were responding to.

Another problem with external inspiration is that it rapidly fades from memory, and we are left with the arduous task of producing our own work with little to go on but a vague feeling of inferiority. This is especially the case with writing which relies on a lot of research, and taking successful notes is therefore vital. This could be as little as a word, phrase, image, or a single line which encapsulates your response to the piece that inspires you. Indeed, don't underestimate the value of physical prompts around you, and how these can contribute to an inspiring setting, studio or workshop space. Natural surroundings can make us feel less stressed and prompt a greater sense of wellbeing[32], so are likely to be beneficial for creativity too. A work space surrounded by inspiring comments and quotes could be very motivating, and increases the likelihood of chance connections coming to mind (See **Strategy 3**).

We can also get inspiration from discussing ideas with peers, i.e. our fellow creatives. Indeed, human creativity may be essentially a social process. Keith Sawyer – a former student and colleague of 'flow' researcher Csikszentmihalyi – feels that creativity works better in groups than individually. We appear to be better at thinking of new ideas when in company, and a group of people are also likely to be more original than are their constituent individuals[33]. A real-world example of these synergistic benefits is how creative The Beatles were when working together, compared with their (arguably) more limited solo work.

On the other hand, people can at times be a distraction, interrupting your train of thought (see **Strategy 4**). As Terese Amabile and Steven Kramer noted in their classic study of creativity in the workplace, the social environment is a major determinant of creativity and provides the motivation to be cre-ative, but its effects can be either positive or negative. Negative effects could arise from a conservative workplace culture, an over-critical attitude from managers, or a lack of procedures for developing new ideas[34]. Similarly, social stress can affect your creativity level, and therefore being in a position where you are likely to be judged could stifle your motivation.

When it comes to getting feedback on your work, the value of social interaction becomes clear, for a reviewer or peer can provide judgements with more objective distance. Some types of project may have external input built into the process – a public art show, reviews of written works, and so on – but in other cases, you might need to arrange feedback for yourself. How you feel about when and how to do this may depend partly on personality, with extraverts feeding off social interaction, and introverts much happier to polish their ideas in solitude, only sharing when they feel a piece is as close as possible to finished. There is little point in trying to fit into a way of working that doesn't suit your personality, not least because personality is thought to be largely innate[35]. It's worth noting that most people actually fall towards the middle of the introvert-extravert scale, one of the key personality factors recognised in psychology (people who are at or close to this midpoint are termed 'ambiverts').

In work settings, we may not always have a choice about who to work with and when, but we can at least choose to focus our creative efforts during times that better suit our needs. There are plenty of teams and groups that don't work well together, simply because certain personalities don't gel (and, of course, some co-workers are simply very annoying!). Particular conditions need to be in place for a group 'flow state' to occur. A really large group increases the chances of a personality clash – the more people there are, the less likely it is that everyone is going to work successfully together.

Key tips:

- Who inspires you? Whether it is an acquaintance or someone that you admire from a greater distance, exposure to great creative work can be both intellectually and emotionally stimulating.
- Identify your preferences for feedback – this is important for all creative work, but do you prefer to share ideas early or wait until later? Either way, it will be important to get feedback at some point.
- Find ways of making the most of social interactions in your setting. If you feel your creativity is being stifled by colleagues or collaborators, focus your creative efforts during time away from these settings – or change them if you can.

Strategy 6: Changing your Location

"I walk making up phrases; sit, contriving scenes"
Virginia Woolf, writer.[36]

Many people have a particular place where they do their creative work – a desk, music room, art studio or wherever. If you are lucky enough to have somewhere that you can work undisturbed, this can help you to reach a state of flow as discussed earlier, and can be set up with inspiring quotes and references to the works of others. Children's author Roald Dahl was known for his habit of working in a shed at the bottom of the garden, while many artists rely on their studio space.

However, there is reason to believe that rather than staying in one preferred place, it can be beneficial to move around – at least for some parts of the creative process. Again, this is partly due to the way memory works – different surroundings naturally triggers different associations, and so changing location both helps us to recall more, and trigger a greater number of new ideas or links. Essentially, associative processes (see **Strategy 3**) are boosted by a wider variety of "input" to your mind.

As creativity involves taking a sideways step out of the habits that the human mind tends to fall into, being continually surrounded by the same places and information can be unhelpful. It makes it harder to avoid the well-trodden path of mental habits. We may even cease to notice many aspects of familiar surroundings after a while. So, although it is comfortable to study, work and do our thinking all in the same place, it is unlikely to be helpful to work this way all of the time. It's worth noting that while many artists are associated with a particular place (the Beatles' favoured Abbey Road studio, for example), they didn't necessarily come up with all of their ideas there.

There is some evidence that even the act of movement itself, for example walking around, may be beneficial to creativity. Anecdotally, many creative writers swear by it; the great English author Charles Dickens took long walks around London by night when devising his characters and plots, and philosopher Friedrich Nietzsche once said, "All truly great thoughts are conceived while walking"[37]. In the research literature, one experimental study by Marily Oppezzo and Daniel Schwartz compared two groups of people, one moving on a treadmill and the other sitting. Both groups were given puzzles and tasks, including Guilford's alternative uses test. They found that although walking had no effect on puzzles and problem solving, it did boost scores on Guilford's creativity test [38]. And of course, a treadmill doesn't even gain the benefits of changing surroundings.

This matter is far from settled scientifically, but it certainly wouldn't do any harm to your creative process (or your physical health) to try out 'creative walking' more often, particularly during stages of a project when you need to develop new ideas. It's possible that other activities such as swimming or jogging have similar effects, allowing the mind to reach an almost meditative state, but activities which occupy a lot of the mind's working memory and attention (such as most competitive sports) are unlikely to have the same benefits.

Moving may also increase the likelihood of seeing new things that we wouldn't see if we stayed at a desk or in a studio. This can lead to an interesting set of ideas or images that can be used in later work. (For example, as I write this section, I'm on a train to Manchester, England. There is a couple standing on the train, deep in conversation. The man is swaying from side to side as he stands, and over his shoulder is a cloth bag saying 'Riba' This puts me in mind of the Czech word 'Ryba', meaning fish).

One exercise sometimes used by people who are learning to write poetry is to go about their normal day, thinking of images or similes for everything they see. So, for example, you see a coin on the ground and think "that's like a brown bug", or see a crumpled plastic bag and think "that looks someone's face when they're crying".

If this seems far removed from workplace or science projects, there are examples of how location can stimulate thinking in those domains, too. Most famously, Archimedes made his 'Eureka' breakthrough in the bath. A less well-known story is how the great German chemist Kekule came up with his prize-winning breakthrough about the ring-shaped structure of benzine (an important chemical component of many oils, knowledge of which was essential for the development of plastics). Kekule explained that during a short break away from the lab, he had a daydream about a snake eating its own tail – and this triggered the idea of benzine's ring shaped structure. With this 'flash of insight' story (as with that of Archimedes) it's important to note that Kekule was an expert scientist, and had been working intensively on the problem in his lab for several weeks. In other words, his mind was primed, but he hadn't yet made the key breakthrough. The idea came to him when he went for a walk through a forest, giving him time to relax, think through images and ideas, and form novel associations with his surroundings.

Actually, Kekule's example might not be all that unusual. Indeed creativity is often considered to progress through a set of stages, including *preparation*, *incubation* and *insight*. Preparation is where we carry out the learning and thinking that gets the mind ready to have a useful idea. Incubation means taking time away from a problem; like a hen sitting on an egg, a period of time passes with nothing much (on the surface) happening. Then comes the breakthrough, the insight moment. This idea dates back to the 1920s work of Graham Wallas, a social psychologist and co-founder of the London School of Economics. It may lack detail, but there remains general agreement with the importance of incubation as a concept[39]. As a delay can help with creative insight or finding a solution, building in breaks, walks, and time away from intractable problems is good creative practice (see **Section 19** for a further research example of incubation).

The benefits of a change of setting may be partly due to forgetting of habits. Psychologically, the more our current context differs from where something was learned, the less readily that information comes to mind, because the memory depends on links and connections that are formed during the learning process, as discussed earlier. A great example of how hard it is to retrieve information out of context is the experience of seeing an acquaintance in a place where we don't normally see that person, and finding it very hard at first to put a name to the face.

However, the shoe is on the other foot when it comes to redrafting or improving on creative ideas or earlier versions of your work. Different contexts make it much harder it is to apply learned skills and strategies to new tasks [40]. There is, therefore, a conflict or tension here – on the one hand, new locations can help to stimulate ideas, but they can also make it harder to use learned skills. Familiar and comfortable work space can help to stimulate flow states and can boost our mood, but new interactions and conversations provide helpful stimuli, and prevent our getting too physically or mentally comfortable.

The obvious solution to this is to intermix novel and familiar locations appropriately – something which may be at least partly a matter of judgement and introspection. When we need an injection of ideas or simply recognise that a change would be beneficial and that we are stuck in a rut, it's time to move, taking a break or a walk. On the other hand, don't interrupt a successful creative task if it's going well. Your workspace is still going to be invaluable for some stages of the creative process, particularly editing and refining the final stages of a project once the insight moment has already occurred.

Key tips:

- Depart from your usual route and habitual places from time to time, and try working in a variety of surroundings, especially while in the early stages of creative projects.
- Use the comfort of familiar surroundings to work without distractions, for example when getting through tricky pieces of work or for editing/reviewing earlier ideas or drafts.
- If you find yourself getting stuck in a rut, try changing position, posture, or going for a walk.

Strategy 7: Lateral Thinking and the Power of Analogy

"Lateral thinking is concerned with breaking out of the concept prisons of old ideas"
  Edward de Bono, researcher.[41]

Is there a creative part of the brain? It's not hard to find inaccurate pseudo-science about left and right brains (also known as two sides of the same brain!), or about some people being visual thinkers and others being verbal thinkers. These ideas are not supported by scientific research. In fact, there are numerous interconnected brain areas involved in any aspect of thinking.

It's true that in most people, language processing is sited particularly in one hemisphere of the brain, leading to major language problems if this area is damaged by an injury. However, it's not the case that creativity is sited particularly in one half of the brain. You couldn't do tasks just with your 'right brain' even if you tried, as complex tasks draw on a large number of brain areas. You certainly want all of the facilities of your creative brain working in harmony, and your brain in general to be in good health (see **Strategy 19**).

Regarding the idea of being a particularly 'visual' or 'verbal' person, there is of course variation among individuals in terms of how good they are at language or imagery, just as some people are better than others at everything. A more useful finding, however, is that people who learn using both words and images together are later better able to recall that information than these who learn through words alone – a phenomenon known as *dual coding*[42]. This suggests that rather than attempting to find our strongest suit, we should all be finding ways of integrating multiple types of sensory experience within our learning and practice.

Perhaps this is why novels which engage the senses are often much more engaging than scientific papers which talk on a factual level, and tend to be dismissed as 'dry'. Indeed, in both your learning and your creative thinking, it would be good practice to use the senses more. Even visual media such as photography and art can seek to elicit other types of sensory experiences.

Regardless of the brain areas involved, psychologists and philosophers do tend to agree that there are different thinking skills. Two of the most important are known as *deductive reasoning* and *inductive reasoning.* The former involves moving from a rule or assumption (or several) to a conclusion/deduction. For example: all birds have beaks, a flub is a type of bird, therefore a flub must have a beak. A good example of this type of reasoning in practice is the popular logic puzzles that involve ruling out options based on factual statements, rather like a detective would rule out suspects in a case.

Inductive reasoning, on the other hand, involves more un- certainty, and may therefore link more with creative processes as well as our appreciation of creativity. How, for example, do we learn what blues music involves? Rather than following a set of rules, you have absorbed numerous previous examples as a listener, and are now able to say with reasonable certainty whether a new example fits the genre or not. In a similar way, we learn how a new idea may fit into our work (or not) via having observed or tried out previous examples. And as noted in **Strategy 3**, viewing new examples in an interleaved, mixed-up order may be especially helpful, as doing so makes it easier to notice subtle differences.

Another alternative to logical, deductive thinking is what psychologist and philosopher Edward de Bono termed *lateral thinking*. In his view, it was essential to avoid habits of thought, as these can lead to errors and biases, making it harder to come up with new ideas. Lateral thinking actively looks for unusual connections (as in **Strategy 3**), but instead of relying on serendipity, a system or technique can be used [43]. One such technique is the reversal method – where you attempt to view a problem in the opposite way to what is usual. For example, rather than looking at a police officer controlling a traffic, de Bono states that you might look at the traffic as controlling the police officer (p. 143). While apparently absurd, such reversals can lead to insights (perhaps the police officer actually is being controlled by the traffic, in a sense), and more importantly, the process helps to free us from lazy habits of thought. Lateral thinking is sometimes nicknamed 'thinking outside the box'.

Lateral thinking relies on the human mind's potential for analogy, that is, making a link between one meaningful idea and another. Analogy is woven through our culture and language, and seems to be the basis of much of human language. A brilliant example of this, raised by the linguist Jean Aitchison, is the case of the word 'buff'. She notes that from the word buffalo, the word buffe gradually came to mean leather, to describe buffalo hides. From there, the word 'buff' came to mean naked (as in skin), and was also used to describe soft leather, from where we obtained the verb to buff (polish) as well as buff-coloured (yellow-brown, the colour of leather but nowadays more often used to describe envelopes). This colour association led to a nickname for NYC volunteer firefighters with yellow uniforms, and from there a 'buff' could mean anyone who volunteers or is enthusiastic about something, such as a film buff [44].

As mentioned in **Strategy 3**, the process of applying strategies to new situations is called transfer, and this has been described as fundamental to all of education[45]. Indeed, transfer is a building block of creativity, as creativity requires – among other things – an ability to apply what we know in an unfamiliar way. What can trigger the insight, or moment where we make a new creative connection? One of the most widely studied techniques is the analogy. Essentially, this involves transferring an idea from one context to another.

Researcher Allison Jaeger and colleagues conducted an experiment looking at how school pupils learned from analogies in science, for example, the idea that the structure of an atom is like the structure of the solar system. Benefiting from an analogy like this typically involves three key stages – remembering the previously learned information, making connections between the right bits of the two similar concepts, and finally transferring ideas from one to the other. Interestingly, they found that learners often needed to see the two ideas simultaneously to make the connection. Children with good visual working memory abilities gained less from being provided with the analogous example simultaneously, perhaps because they were better at holding it in mind.

To make use of analogies in your creative work, it's necessary to allow yourself the thinking time to see how ideas (or concepts, techniques, characters, etc) may apply out of context. As with lateral thinking, this involves stepping away from habits of mind and looking for new connections. But it's worth bearing in mind how valuable it is to see the ideas close together. This can happen by chance, but (as mentioned in **Strategy 3**), it will be beneficial to look at old materials regularly to help prompt a connection. When relying on a body of previous work to inspire your current project, don't over-rely on memory (which is always fallible), but revisit that material, and keep it to hand in your workspace. It's also valuable to deliberately avoid habits of mind when creating, even if this leads to a less smooth creative process in the short term.

Key tips:

- Don't pay attention to pseudoscience about different sides/areas of the brain or learning styles, but instead try to use multiple senses when learning and when thinking creatively.
- Creative thinking can be guided by multiple examples (inductive reasoning) and benefits from (lateral thinking).
- Making analogies is easier when we can see two similar concepts side by side. In practice, this could mean keeping your sources of inspiration close at hand.

Strategy 8: Tapping into the Unconscious

"You are not, and cannot become, consciously aware of most of your brain's ongoing activities."
    Leda Cosmides and John Tooby, psychologists.[46]

While some aspects of the creativity can be deliberately primed and leveraged using strategies described previously, there may well be aspects of our creativity involve processes that we are not even aware of. Some, in effect, operate when we are not even thinking about the task at hand. As such, they are difficult to control, influence or improve.

There are different theories in psychology about why unconscious thought processes might occur – some of which are controversial. Carl Jung, for example, thought that the mind drew on a *collective unconscious* of cultural knowledge. Sigmund Freud said that much of the mind is 'beneath the surface' of our conscious awareness. By his analogy, the conscious mind is like a fountain in the sunshine, while the unconscious is the large and forceful reservoir that it draws upon. He encouraged his patients to 'free associate', letting one idea flow onto another to reveal unconscious thoughts and desires[47].

Although these early theories are nowadays seen as deeply flawed, the general principle that some thought processes occur without awareness – and that they can be significant – has received some support from modern cognitive psychology and behavioural neuroscience. For example, a great many memory and learning processes can and do happen without us making a conscious effort to remember things. One example is a process called priming – things such as faces and music seem more appealing to us if we have experienced them before, even if we have no conscious recollection of them whatsoever. The *mere exposure effect*, studied by psychologist Robert Zajonc in the 1960s, showed that this extends even to words – people show a preference for words that they have heard recently[48]. This may be in part because we have an innate tendency to be wary and fearful of things that are unfamiliar.

A great deal of our learning of vocabulary happens through similar implicit, incidental processes – we don't learn words one-by-one through deliberate study[49]. Indeed, some psychology researchers believe that a lot of our daily thought processes happen largely automatically. Tanya Chartrand and John Bargh are perhaps best known for demonstrating the 'chameleon effect' – the finding that we unconsciously mimic others' body language – especially that of people we like[50]. In their 1999 article, *The unbearable automaticity of being*, the pair argue that "most of a person's everyday life is determined not by their conscious intentions and deliberate choices but... operate outside of conscious awareness and guidance"[51]. What this means in practice is that many of our daily actions may be largely automatic. A way of looking at this is to imagine your attention as a spotlight, focusing on different things at any given time. If a task is easy and routine – brushing your teeth, dressing, driving along a simple route – then this spotlight, our attention, can focus on other things (this also means that bad habits can be automatic, and difficult to correct – for example, grammatical errors). Likewise, the bulk of our long-term memories are, almost by definition, not in our conscious mind at any given moment.

What exactly are the role of automatic or unconscious processes in creativity? The unconscious is undoubtedly a store-house of material, but interesting associations can't be taken for granted. Given how much happens without conscious awareness, it's likely that some key decisions – if not the entire process – are happening on autopilot, and this could lead to some stale, obvious choices being selected. It may be helpful to focus on the outcome of this automatic processing by slowing down, reviewing, and considering the decisions that you have made. Where necessary, tackle the automatic choices by deliberately rethinking – rather than going with the first idea that springs to mind, try the second or the third. How is your work looking now?

It is likely that some associative processes also happen without our awareness, and this could even be one of the purposes of dreams – recoding, consolidating, amending and synthesising the day's thoughts and experiences. Although it was once thought that the purpose of dreaming was to delete the clutter from the brain's storage systems[52], it is now known that sleep can strengthen memory and boost problem solving. So sleeping on a problem really could help (the power of napping is further discussed in **Strategy 9**).

Freewriting is the author's equivalent of Sigmund Freud's therapy of free association. Essentially freewriting it means letting one idea lead to another, without trying to consciously guide the process. Why might this work? Rather than revealing hidden desires, modern psychologists would probably suggest that this is a way of switching off the conscious processes which direct and oversee human thought – a set of functions known as metacognition, or thinking about thinking. By switching off your inner critic, that part that thinks about what you are writing and whether it is good or not, a broader and less self-conscious set of information is likely to emerge. Again, much of this is likely to be very poor writing, but by dredging up a mixture of thoughts and memories without planning or editing, the method has potential get a more interesting mix of ideas, rather like the process of brainstorming, which may then stimulate useful associations at a later stage.

Key tips:

- Unconscious thought processes have a role to play in creativity, but can also lead to stale and obvious associations.
- Tackle automatic processing by slowing down, reviewing, and focusing on why you have made certain choices.
- Try freewriting – the writing itself will be poor quality, but some of the themes or images could be worth exploring further, and the process may help you to temporarily switch off your inner critic.

Strategy 9: Take a Power Nap

*"Sleep not only rights the wrong of prolonged wakeful-
ness but, at a neurocognitive level, it moves you beyond
where you were before you took a nap."*
   Matthew Walker, researcher.[53]

A s noted in the previous section, sleep can play a role
in developing ideas and forming new associations. In
recent years, there has been increasing interest in the
role of napping. Can a short (sometimes very short) nap have
genuine benefits to our thought processes?

One thing that is clear is that having a rest can boost certain
mental abilities, while, of course, a lengthy time spent awake
can be harmful for concentration. Staying awake for 17 hours
can lead to an equivalent effect on focused performance to
having a 0.05% blood alcohol-level[54] – above the legal limit
for driving in most countries – and being more sleep deprived
than that can lead to major risks for mental and physical health,
increase your chance of falling asleep at the wheel when driving,
and can even cause hallucinations.

In terms of our cognitive (mental) abilities, researchers know
that decreases in attention and working memory performance

can be linked to poor sleep[55]. Sleep is also important for learning; babies nap throughout the day because they are learning so much and their brains are developing. Fatigue can make you poorer at problem solving and even at sports (perhaps because of the concentration required).

Tiredness therefore makes it harder to stay focused and reduces the mind's ability to engage with many of the skills required in your creative work. It's not impossible to produce good work when tired; in his essay *On Writing*, Raymond Carver discusses how his early years as an author involved writing for an hour per evening after his day job and family duties. However, he also notes that his choice of short stories rather than novels as a writing form was in part due to the fact that he simply wouldn't have been capable of a novel under such circumstances[56].

A nap has potential to improve focus, and in many countries, it is normal to take some form of siesta midway through the day. Some people have experimented with taking this further, having a couple of naps and a reduced main period of sleep as a form of 'polyphasic' sleeping pattern[57]. In fact, the idea of having a single 7-8 hour block of sleep may be something of a modern invention, stimulated by the development of electrical lighting; our ancestors would wake in the night to write or complete tasks [58], and our close cousins the great apes nap during the day[59].

A number of research studies have looked at the effects of naps on performance, including creativity. People appear to have better all-around cognitive abilities after a short nap. Numerous studies have found that a short nap (20 minutes or less – often called a *power nap*) can boost focus and productivity for the next couple of hours. A longer nap can have benefits which are slightly more long lasting[60], but it could be argued that this is less time-efficient overall, not least because it takes longer to fully wake up and get to work after you have been in a deep sleep. Curiously, drinking a caffeinated drink just before taking a nap can be beneficial, because the caffeine takes effect too slowly to affect the nap, and instead coincides with when the napper wants to wake up, helping a more rapid cognitive recovery. This power-nap/coffee combination has been nicknamed a 'nappuccino'[61], and has been shown to help combat sleepiness in drivers. It could certainly help with long shifts of creative work, too.

Tackling this issue from another angle, what happens if habitual nappers are prevented from napping? A study by Taotao Ru and colleagues from South China Normal University looked at students who habitually took a nap at around midday. When prevented from doing so, the students performed worse in tests of working memory, sustained attention (being able to focus for a period of time), and in tasks that require metacognition (the ability to keep track of your own strategies and progress). Their mood wasn't significantly harmed and neither was their reaction time, but clearly their ability to mentally engage in anything complex will have been reduced.

It might seem strange that a short nap could really affect anything, given that a full 'sleep cycle' (during which the brain moves from light to deep sleep, followed by a period of 'rapid eye movement' dream sleep) lasts for 90-120 minutes. The benefits are largely felt in a person's increased focus and attention, but it could also be the case that by briefly dropping off, we initiate some of the associative processes that the brain uses to consolidate memories during the 'rapid eye movement' phase of sleep.

Surprisingly, it's also possible that the slight disorientation most people feel after waking from sleep or from a nap could be helpful to creative tasks. Research by sleep scientists Björn Rasch and Jan Born found that people who napped woke up in a 'hyperassociative' phase, which may have links to dream sleep[62]. This openness to connections and associations could be an excellent time for brainstorming, and for developing and making links among a set of initial ideas. It is possible that sleepiness is functioning to switch off some of our usual tendency to edit or follow routines when thinking. Therefore brainstorming, freewriting, or sketching out new ideas could be excellent tasks to do first thing in the morning, with the sleepy state reducing the tendency for overthinking about our work.

Ultimately it may be a matter of personal choice as to whether napping could work for you. This is area of research is still developing, and not much is known about the long-term effects of regular naps, or of interrupting naps after a few minutes. It might be safest to take the length of nap that you feel most comfortable with, if you do it all. And of course, some people simply don't have the necessary space – or peace and quiet – during the day. Others may have the opportunity but either find it difficult to drop off, or just find the whole process unpleasant! It's also generally not advisable to nap too late in the day, because doing so can impact on your main sleep, making issues such as insomnia more likely.

Key tips:

- Avoid trying to produce important work when you are tired, as the effects of fatigue seriously reduce performance.
- Try power naps lasting 15-20 minutes for a quick boost to attention and cognitive abilities without the recovery times associated with longer naps, but opt for longer naps if these

feel more comfortable to you.

- If you drink it, experiment with a strong coffee or similar caffeinated drink just before a nap.

Strategy 10: Revising Work with Fresh Eyes

"In notebooks and in her head, there was Harry Potter. She could not leave the idea alone, and it would not leave her."

Lindsay Fraser, biographer of J. K. Rowling.[63]

A simple and highly effective strategy for developing and refining any kind of creative work is to take a break, preferably for several days, during the process. As well as providing some objective distance when judging the quality of your own work so far, a bit of time out can also help you to come up with new ideas to develop. Research into memory shows that by spacing out practice of skills or revision, we remember it better than if practice was more intensive. This so-called *distributed practice* is also more effective the longer you need to remember the information. This may be at least partly because when looking at the material at different times, we form different associations and are in a different frame of mind. Effectively, the two well-spaced-out learning sessions are recalled as two separate but linked events in the mind[64].

This spacing effect helps with remembering facts, but it can also play a role in developing understanding and generalising from what we've learned[65]. Creative work and our ability to transfer knowledge and skills can therefore benefit from it, too. There are diminishing returns of continuing to chip away at one task or issue, and benefits to the creative process of returning to it after a short delay, with new enthusiasm. In any case, most major creative projects will take many days, and allowing sufficient time and being tolerant of slow progress will be more helpful in the long run than impatience or haste. However, don't leave the project to one side for so long that you have largely forgotten the details and the main emotions that motivated it in the first place, or simply procrastinate while leaving key jobs unfinished! More than a few weeks and things will start to get harder, not easier, to finish.

Gaps between different projects may also give time for new ideas, feelings and knowledge that can feed into your work and help you to build your long-term career progress as a creative professional. In his TED talk *The Power of Time Off* which has been viewed over 2 million times, designer Stefan Sagmeister describes how he closes down his team for several days, forcibly taking them away from a project to refresh their minds, and then reengaging with it. Sagmeister describes how his team's creative work was tending to become stuck in a rut, and how time out was not merely a break but helped to inspired successful new spin-off projects.

This option won't be available to many of us when it comes to the day job, but from the point of view of a creative task, one way to achieve this kind of lengthy break is to change your focus for a few weeks after completing a large project, devoting your attentions and energy into new learning, new challenges or background research. This will help with motivation, and also means that the development of skills and knowledge (see **Strategy 2**) will be interspersed with using those skills creatively. To use a popular analogy, you can't keep taking from the well without giving it time to refill.

A delay could also be beneficial once the early creative and drafting processes are complete. At this stage, a larger delay could be useful, so that the details really have been forgotten. This can allow you to act more like a reviewer or editor of your own work. As noted earlier (see **Strategy 5**), it is valuable in any creative endeavour to receive feedback from others. It's all too easy to get caught up in a project and fail to recognise its flaws, and hard to appreciate how something may look or sound to an external audience – a critical friend or colleague can provide this judgement with a more objective distance. By leaving a (preferably almost finished) project aside for a few weeks or months, you can generate your own feedback by looking at work with 'fresh eyes'.

You can also create a sense of emotional distance via a time delay, which could be very useful to boost your criticality. The effect of this appears to depend on how much we mentally detach ourselves from previous events. A fascinating research study by psychologists Cindy Ward and Anne Wilson at Wilfrid Laurier University in Ontario found that if a person was reflecting on their own past behaviour, they were more likely to be critical if the phrasing of a question made the event seem more distant. If participants were asked about an event "all the way back at the beginning of the term", they were more likely to be harsh than those who were asked about events "in the recent past, at the beginning of the term", even though the time referred to was the same. This shows that a psychological sense of distance, rather than the mere passing of time, allows us to be more objective and critical.

It follows that re-visiting your work after a delay can allow you to critique and evaluate it more soberly. Seeing your own work again after the initial project excitement has worn off allows you to perceive it afresh, almost as an external audience would. The exact time delay will depend on your own attachment to the project, and pragmatic considerations will also play a role – most people are working to deadlines of some kind. Some writers swear by putting items into their desk drawer (or pen-drive, cloud, etc) when writing an article or chapter, but this may not be practical for the journalist whose work is due in a few days or less. In terms of critically reviewing your own work, though, the longer you can leave it, though, the better, allowing some forgetting and emotional detachment to come into play.

Exactly what and how quickly you forget is actually very interesting. The mind is good at remembering gist i.e. the meaning of an experience or text, and poorer at recalling precise detail, which is why people who tell a joke or repeat an anecdote tend not to use exactly the same words as before (and sometimes we may find ourselves thinking 'this sounded better when I heard it'!). Additionally, if you look at a creative piece repeatedly, the detail becomes so familiar that perceiving it is almost automatic – the mind knows what to expect, so it saves itself the effort and takes a short cut. When re-reading, for example, we barely focus on the words at all by the fourth or fifth reading, easily skim-reading the text. This effect is even stronger with a musical or visual piece, because the human mind is so good at remembering music and pictures.

The speed of forgetting also depends on how good your memory is, which varies between individuals. This is an area that therefore needs to be experimented with in your own practice, but it is important to build one or more delay into the planning process from the start (see **Strategy 15**), rather than completing your work too close to the deadline.

In sum then, a short delay is beneficial to refresh your creative process mid-way through, but this mustn't be too long. The 'desk drawer' technique, on the other hand, should occur *after* the bulk of the creative work is complete. This can't be over-stated – if you leave an unfinished work to finish after a period of months or years, it may never get done, and it will feel almost like starting from scratch with new ideas when you return to it. And it may well be the case that your future self has other priorities! Even if you do go back to the work, your mood and sense of purpose will have changed, leading to the sense that you are trying to finish someone else's project.

Key tips:

- Take a short break of a day or a few days to experience the benefits of incubation of ideas and to come back refreshed and newly motivated.
- Make use of much longer breaks by placing projects in a 'desk drawer', then re-visiting them more like an objective audience would do.
- Don't put projects aside for a long period without completing at least one full draft first.

Bonus Strategy: Setting Limits and Constraints

"the willow tree / I had never noticed / before this grey rainy day"
Haiku by Alan Spence.[66]

W hen I planned this book I intended to have ten chapters in each section – a form of constraint on my own creativity. But sometimes you need to bend the rules a little, and limits can stimulate new ideas!

It may seem that having no limits on what you can do or produce would be a very good thing, freeing you up to create anything you like. However, it actually fits very well with the points made so far (for example, about connections to existing ideas, or about using categories to brainstorm) if you *don't* start with nothing. If you do, you have nothing to which to link your ideas, and no mental categories to draw upon. Although constraints may seem at first to be unappealing, they can be a way of breaking up the creative blockage that arises from an unplanned day or a blank page.

A constraint is anything that limits what we can do or produce, or how we go about our creative work. In fact, there are already many constraints inherent in most creative fields and projects, even if we don't always think about them. For example, a photographer is constrained by the rectangular shape of a photograph, and a painter is constrained by the physical characteristics of their materials.

Unintuitively, many artists have found that increasing the level of constraints – rather than reducing them – has boosted their level of originality. For example, the Oulipo group (or *ouvroir de literature potentielle*, i.e. "workshop of potential literature") set out to discover new forms of writing by setting themselves challenges to overcome. One writer from the group, George Perec, produced a lengthy poem in which each line is an anagram, as well as a novel that does not include the letter 'e', and a 5,000-letter palindrome[67]!

On a more everyday level, a person's choices inevitably constrain them. Are you choosing to make a short film, or write a sonnet, conduct a research project on animals, or take photographs only in black and white? Any such choice places constraints on what we can or can't do right from the outset.

While constraints are certainly limiting, there may be a psychological rationale as to why they have a beneficial effect. In their 1972 book 'Human problem solving', Allen Newell and Herbert Simon explain that when we solve problems, we move from the *starting state* (for example, a blank sheet of paper) to the *goal state* (for example, a new product to take to market). To do so, we have to navigate past all of the possible intermediate states and moves that comprise what they call *problem space*[68].

When it comes to solving a traditional logic problem, there is only one correct answer, and it is therefore beneficial to reduce the problem space by getting rid of irrelevant options, and avoiding going down dead ends. A creative problem is different in that there are multiple possible solutions. Nevertheless, it makes sense that simple constraints can lead us to think our way more efficiently from the starting state to one possible goal state. Any such constraint reduces the size of the problem space, making it more manageable to think through the options.

One way of picturing how hard it is to think through all of the options in a problem space is to imagine playing a game of chess. After each move by your opponent, there are multiple possible moves that you could make in response, and each of these moves in turn lead to multiple possibilities. It's easy to see that across a whole game, the number of possible moves and their consequences becomes enormous. Indeed, only recently have computers become powerful enough to compute all of the possible moves in a chess game and their consequences, and therefore to work out the most likely winning strategy in any given situation.

Human players, of course, do not actually think through the consequences of every possible move. Instead they reduce the size of the problem space using *heuristics*. Heuristics are mental shortcuts, such as 'always avoid losing your queen' or 'never lose a piece without gaining anything', and these vastly reduce the number of moves a player could choose to make.

In other creative fields (after all, chess and other games could be seen as creative, too!), there are similar mental shortcuts. In business, there may be constraints placed upon you by a client, such as a deadline. Filmmakers may need to consider the type of content that can or cannot be included depending on the age of the audience.

In your own work, it may actually be useful for you to map out the starting state, problem space and goal state for your current project on a piece of paper or computer document. It could be represented as a flow chart, with arrows leading to multiple areas of the problem space. You can then start to think of ways of reducing the problem space via heuristics and through drawing on experience. As with chess players, it's simply not possible to work through all of the options. If you find it hard to make decisions about which avenues to go down, take a leaf out of the Oulipo group's book (and that of the Dada poets) and simply choose randomly (see **Strategy 3**).

In some fields and in some parts of the world, there are religious or legal limits to what creative artists are allowed to produce, and again, this can lead to surprising or counterintuitive benefits. For Islamic art in medieval times, the rule against idolatry – i.e. portraying images of people – led to some of the stunning geometric art forms which are best exemplified by the Alhambra in Moorish Spain, versions of which are seen in mosques around the world to this day. It's arguably no great coincidence that some of the finest poetry of the 20th century was written by poets in Eastern Europe under Communism, and by Irish writers responding to social and political turmoil. The poetry itself was a creative response, a way of overcoming a constraint: the fact that they could not openly say what they thought about the political regime in their country[69].

Given that the problem space is already constrained by our field (for example, TV advertising), by the requirements of the task (for example, producing a 20-second video advert) and by other factors (budget, timescale, and so forth), does it make sense to constrain ourselves further? Why, for example, would it be a good idea for an advertising creative to say "I will put a dog into the advert, film it entirely from above, and not have anyone speaking in English"?

One way of making sense of this is to say that each constraint is actually a new idea that can stimulate further ideas, providing a stimulus for creative thinking. In a way, it divides a vast problem space into something that is specific and manageable. Like the categories used in brainstorming, such limitations can stimulate and focus our thinking. And like the ideas discussed under **Strategy 3**, it can force us out of mundane habits of mind, and make us find new and unusual connections instead of stale and obvious choices.

Imagine being asked to write an after-dinner speech about one of your closest friends or family members. It is difficult to know where to start – hobbies, food, shared holidays... the list goes on. If, however, you were asked to write about something very specific – how they react to their least-favourite food, for example, it would be much easier to think of a series of anecdotes and examples, helping to stimulate the beginnings of a witty and coherent speech. This also wouldn't stop you bringing in other aspects of your friend's life, but would provide a coherent core idea to which others could be added.

Similarly, think about a time that you have had to work around a problem in your creative work or in your everyday life. Something hasn't gone right, and you have had to deal with it. This is often where ideas come to us in their purest form, and most spontaneously – there is a problem to solve, and we have a set of tools to try and solve it. It's rather like Guilford's alternative uses task, but in a real context.

It would therefore make sense to at least try out adding one or more constraints to your creative work. You could always remove them later! It may be the case that in your field, there are already a set of widely recognised set of constraints that you could immediately put into practice. For example, poets who try writing haiku limit the number of lines and syllables that they use, in contrast to 'free verse' poetry.

However, if you are unsure where to start, then you could try an activity that draws on the spirit of George Perec, and constrain yourself by removing one or more everyday element of your craft. You may need to take a few minutes to think of exactly what everyday elements or tools are taken for granted in your own field or medium (itself a creative task!). For example, a writer could try writing a story with no direct speech, a painter could eschew a particular colour, while a composer could decide not to use a particular musical note. Not all such experiments will lead to useful products in the end, but they may at least prompt you to reconsider and re-evaluate things that had previously been automatic.

Often it is not the constraint itself that leads to good ideas, but your attempts to overcome it. For example, Jimi Hendrix is arguably best known not just for his skill with the guitar (which was undeniably superb) but for his ability to push beyond the limitations of the electric guitar. More generally, Hendrix found new ways of creating sounds and in doing so, he helped to expand the boundaries of rock music in the mid-1960s.

Scottish bagpiper Gordon Duncan likewise extended the usual scope of his instrument. The bagpipes are generally considered to be capable of producing only nine notes, and until recently were used only for traditional Scottish folk tunes. When attempting to play the heavy metal anthem 'Thunderstuck' by AC/DC on the bagpipes, Duncan was forced to find new ways of creating notes and sounds, outside of that traditional scale. In doing so, he inspired a generation of younger pipers, and was thrown out of the Scottish Bagpiping Association, a sequence of events which inspired the play 'Thunderstruck' by David Colvin.

Key tips:

- Write down the existing constraints in your current project or your chosen creative field more generally, for example length/timescale, choice of medium/form/materials, and so forth.
- Visually map out the route from your starting state via the problem space to your goal state.
- Experiment with adding one or more constraint, focusing more on ways of getting around and dealing with that constraint than on the problem or idea itself.

II

CRAFT AND HABITS

This part of the book is about the behaviours and habits involved in day-to-day creative practice. It presents another set of 10 strategies that you can immediately start using to achieve high levels of creative productivity.

Strategies 11–20 focus on how we can treat our creative activities as a craft, tending to each idea and piece of work like a patient gardener tends to plants, doing a little every now and again but also finding the motivation to put in the long hours of hard work.

Strategy 11: Getting Going and Staying on Task

"Life is easy to chronicle, but bewildering to practice."
    E. M. Forster, novelist.[70]

It's not easy to get started on a lengthy and complex task, and sometimes even harder to stay on task once things start to get messy and the stakes (success or failure of the whole project?) start to rise. Every decision may start to seem both difficult and threatening. At such times, it's easy to get demotivated, or to start to feel down or anxious. It's also all too easy to get sidetracked with other projects. These will probably seem appealing simple and fresh compared to what you've been working on for many weeks!

Mood is one of the hardest things for any creative professional to manage. Who hasn't felt, from time to time, that despite all the hard work, things are just not going the way that you had hoped – the whole project seems doomed to fail, and you might as well scrap the whole thing and give up? And who hasn't had the experience of feeling tired and demotivated, so that the last thing you want to do is struggle on a little further with a project which is still less than halfway finished? It's like being a few miles into a marathon – the initial excitement has waned, and you are still a long way from the finish line! Normal as these feelings are, they are fundamentally problems with motivation, and can be tackled using evidence from psychology.

One key tip is to create a bit of separation between the work and your identity. This is hard to do because, on some level, creatives do get judged on what they produce. Your creative projects might be a fundamental part of who you are, and may even be the thing you value most about yourself as a person.

Nevertheless, it is possible to modify how you view a creative project and its outcome. An unhelpful *fixed mindset* is where you see each success or failure as reflecting on your ability – the project was a failure, so therefore you feel like a failure, too. Much more useful and better for both your motivation and your mental health is to develop a *growth mindset* about your work. From this point of view, a failure is seen as a useful learning process, allowing you to take one step forward in your own experience and skill [71]. In effect, this allows you to develop the kind of mental separation between art and artist where a critical review doesn't cut you to the quick, but is taken as a worthwhile comment which you can take on board and may be able to learn from (see also **Strategy 10**, regarding developing your own objective self-criticism by using delays).

Motivation has been widely studied by psychologists, and although it is hard to manage in a group or workplace situation, it's much easier for you as an individual to identify and leverage the things that motivate you. One of the key distinctions is between intrinsic and extrinsic motivation:

- *Intrinsic motivation* is inherent in the task, that is, enjoying something for its own sake.
- *Extrinsic motivation* is based on external reward. It means

doing something primarily because you want the outcome that will result from having completed the task.

In practice, it's a little more complex than that. These two types of motivation could both play a role in the same project, coming to the fore at different times. In the case of writers, for example, perhaps you really enjoy writing but can't stand editing. In that case, penning your first draft will be intrinsically motivating – pleasurable in and of itself – but later stages may require more of an external push. This could come from an impending deadline – perhaps you promised to get the work in by a particular date? – or from the pleasure of sending the work off to your agent or publisher, or perhaps from an anticipated payment or royalty. It might be possible (or necessary) to 'hack' your extrinsic motivation by rewarding yourself – a night off for every 5000 words edited, for example.

A good working space can be motivating (notwithstanding the benefits of moving around – see **Strategy 7**), both in terms of having an appealing place to work, and actual physical comfort (which is intrinsically motivating). Sometimes, it may be helpful to find a place that makes distractions impossible; even although I have a desk in the university where I work, for example, I sometimes go to the postgraduate study area to work in silence, away from interruptions, phone calls, or the temptation to chat with a colleague.

Interestingly, it's might not be just the space itself that matters, but how you occupy it. A lot of research suggests that physical posture and the way we sit or stand in a working space can affect both mood and cognitive output. Tensing your muscles can make you more determined[72] but possibly at a cost of increasing psychological and bodily stress, impeding the extent to which we can enter a flow state (we all know how grumpy people feel after a cramped journey, and how hard it is to concentrate if you are too hot or too cold). There is even some research that suggests that faking a smile may make you happier (although attempts to reproduce this finding have been mixed, so the jury is still out on whether putting on an artificial grin is a good idea). Overall, though, there clearly is a two-way connection between our mood and the body.

When it comes to creativity, you can therefore try modifying your sitting or standing position in order to facilitate a relaxed state of mind that will allow you to focus over a period of time. To enter a flow state you need to be both alert and relaxed, and it's probably a good idea to find a physical position that helps you to achieve both of these things. This can be down to individual preference – some people may find it's best to stand or walk around during creative tasks, while others prefer to sit.

Perhaps you should even consider lying down; an experiment by researchers Lypicki & Byrne found that their participants solved complex verbal puzzles better when lying flat on their back compared to sitting or standing. Fans of NBC's series *Mad Men* will be familiar with this image – lead character Don Draper (played by Jon Hamm) is a creative advertising executive who is regularly seen lying on a couch in his office rather than sitting at his desk. It's unclear if it's the change of perspective, pace, posture, or something else, but it may be worth a try to help promote an 'insight' moment, solution or helpful new idea for the issue that you have been puzzling over.

One other key aspect of posture and position is health. Many creatives, whether working with physical materials or at a computer, may find themselves in the same position for many hours. Over the course of months, or indeed years, the effect of poor posture or repetitive movements can begin to be harmful. Insufficient support for example from a chair or desk can move from being a nuisance to a hazard, and in the long term, this could impact on your ability to create. It's worth taking the time to research health issues that are specific to creatives in your field, and investing in quality equipment and furnishings where necessary.

Key tips:

- Consider what aspects of your key creative tasks are intrinsically or extrinsically motivating; when it's the latter, identify extrinsic rewards or social commitments that could help keep projects moving forward.
- Make sure that your own working space that is appealing and that everything comes easily to hand, but also have one or more alternative places where you can work for a change of scene or to get some peace and quiet.
- Consider a change of posture from time to time, and look into ways to promote long term comfort and avert health problems that are typical in your field.

Strategy 12: The Power of a Nudge

"*Solitude sometimes is best society*"
John Milton, writer.[73]

Nudge psychology refers to the power of small changes, pushing rather than forcing us towards desired behaviour. Psychologists are increasingly recognising that small ways of making things easier or, alternatively, more inconvenient can have more of an effect than the large external rewards or punishments that we typically associate with extrinsic motivation.

Often, nudge psychology is deployed by people trying to sell you things, or pondered over by governments who want to minimise vandalism or get people to pay their taxes. You may be aware of your local doctor or dentist sending text message reminders – a simple and cost-effective 'nudge' to stop people missing appointments. Interestingly, such methods are even more effective if they are personalised, such as by sending the same text message with the signature or a member of staff, and with the recipient's first name used as a salutation[74].

The same principles can be applied closer to home. Let's say you are struggling to motivate yourself to clean the bathroom regularly. Storing the cleaning supplies so that they are easily at hand, having spare cloths so that there's always one available, or even just buying more attractive and easier-to-use products – any of these things could provide a nudge.

While strategic changes can helpfully nudge you towards a desired task, it's also important to tackle things that nudge you away from it. Aspects of a situation that make it awkward and uncomfortable can have the opposite effect to those described above, adding to the psychological friction and making it more likely that you will procrastinate. In short, nudge psychology is all about making a desired action easier to do, and cutting out little inconveniences that might discourage you.

To apply this nudge effect to your creative endeavours, you need to make the creative project easy and convenient, and make any distractions really awkward. This will help to ensure that getting the creative work done is the easiest thing to do – anything else is too much trouble!

Remember that a nudge can work in either direction, and there may already be things that are nudging you away from sticking to work schedules. Perhaps the complex set up of your work space is nudging you away from getting on with the work – instead, it should be made very easy to access, so that you can't avoid or fail to think about it. If it's necessary to get your art supplies out of the garage on a weekday evening, it will be all too easy to find something else to do – especially on rainy days. For creatives whose work is computer-based, what about setting yourself a reminder to charge the laptop, so that it's primed and ready to go first thing – right beside the snacks and a comfy chair.

Of course, laptops themselves are full of distractions. Here the nudging away value of hassles and inconveniences can be put productively to work by putting your work-related software front and centre on your desktop, and tucking internet browsers, games and other distractions into a subfolder of a subfolder. A lovely example of this comes from the *Frog and Toad* books of children's writer Arnold Lobel, where the characters find it so hard to stop eating cookies that they put the cookies in a box, tie up the box, and put it on top of a high shelf that requires a ladder to reach (although in the end, even this isn't enough to keep them from temptation!).

If the internet or social media are too much of a distraction, try charging your phone in a harder-to-access part of the house, and perhaps even switching wi-fi off entirely while you work (ideally, this would be done in such a way that it is a nuisance to switch back on – again making the nudge value of a hassle work in your favour).

Identifying other forms of procrastination may require some reflection, as will finding ways to utilise nudges such that these issues are less likely to interfere with your day-to-day creative work. When you stop working on a project and allow a couple of hours to pass, what are you doing? Switching on the TV and getting hooked on the news? Going for lunch with a friend or colleague, and chatting for a couple of hours, or taking a very extended tea break? Many people may not even know what is eating into their time.

For a couple of weeks (ideally 'normal' weeks – not when you are on holiday or on a break from work), keep a diary-style note of your exact movements and the time spent on *all* activities. Include everything – eating, commuting, time in bed, hobbies and sports, even time in the bathroom. Then, after the two weeks is up, plug these times into a spreadsheet and calculate an average of how many minutes and hours you are spending on each task. Could there be any efficiencies made? After all, it's *your* time. How do you want to spend it? (If you find this sort of tracking very difficult to do, a simple hack is to set a timer to ring every 30 minutes, and then note down the last thing you have been doing. There are also apps for this).

These two aspects of nudge psychology can work in tandem – using simple strategies to prompt yourself towards the task at hand, and analysing and obstructing the distractions and time sinks in your life. Obviously, nobody is perfectly time efficient, and you may be entirely comfortable with spending a couple of hours a day chatting on the phone or 30 minutes a day staring out of a train window (indeed, some of this down time may be very helpful for the incubation part of the creative process – see **Strategies 6 & 10**). Small changes such as these don't make essentials such as the internet impossible to access, but they make them less automatic, so that the path of least resistance is to get on with your creative project.

Key tips:

- As far as possible, cut out any hassles or obstructions that get in the way of your creative work, such as by making your work space easier to access, nudging yourself towards your creative project(s).
- Find ways of making distractions harder to access, within reason.
- Take time to analyse how much time you are spending on each of your daily tasks, averaging it across a couple of weeks.

Strategy 13: Nailing Down Good Habits

"Excellence is not an act, but a habit."
Aristotle, philosopher.[75]

W hile creative thinking by its nature is never going to be simple, it will ease the process along if all of the tasks which support and surround your creative practice – the admin involved in submitting your work, cleaning or preparing equipment, tuning instruments, and so forth – become simpler, more familiar and routine, so that they are second nature to you. Ideally, these things will be an almost automatic part of your routine. Easing these more mundane aspects of our creative working life will make everything else a lot less effortful, freeing up that essential attention and working memory capacity, and allowing creative focus where and when it is most needed.

We'd all love to have the kind of awesome creative habits that we sometimes hear about – getting up to work at dawn every day for two hours, perhaps – but such habits are very hard to develop and also hard to stick to. A close friend of mine who is a doctor recently described giving lifestyle advice to patients – he estimated that only around 7% stick to their medical advice on diet and exercise, despite their wholeheartedly agreeing with the plan at the time. There is an extent to which this may sound as if humans are somehow incapable of sticking to their desired routines. But to look at it another way, it also shows the astonishing power of habit. The doctor's patients were sticking to a routine – it's just that it was their old, established routine which won out over the new and healthier plan.

How, then, can we get rid of our bad habits and establish more productive ones? Contrary to popular assumptions, habits take a really long time to establish – from a couple of months at the minimum, up to nearly a year of doing a task every day. Phillippa Lally, a health psychologist at University College London, studied this in the context of establishing healthier dietary habits to reduce cancer risks. In a study originally conducted as part of her PhD, she found that while participants found habit change effortful at first, it became easier over time as the component tasks became more automatic[76]. It was therefore in the initial stage that external nudges and rewards were most needed. She was even able to specify a precise times – 66 days – as the point at which behaviours started to become habitual.

Another finding of the study was that a break from routine such as a holiday tended to lead to a regression in the new habits, and therefore additional effort was needed to reinforce new routines at and after those crunch points. Her research team also found that their participants had more success in establishing diet routines when they were in the workplace – an example of how having an existing routine can act as a scaffold for a new one.

What do you want to do every day in your creative practice? What thing that currently takes a lot of effort would you like to be able to do near-effortlessly in the future? It's important to be realistic. For example, I know that I could be very productive if I got up at 6am every day and spent an hour writing, but I also know that I wouldn't stick to it – over the long term, sufficient sleep is also important! Identify what works for you, working with, not against, your temperament and personality.

Making a personal and public commitment can also be helpful – another form of nudge. Psychologists know that social pressure can be incredibly powerful, prompting people to deny the evidence of their own eyes or say things that they don't actually agree with[77]. Making a public statement to family, friends or colleagues along the lines of "I'm going to complete a new painting every month of this year", "I'm going to write 2000 words per day for a month" is highly motivating, not least because of a general psychological drive to achieve consistency between what we say and what we do.

This effect of a public commitment is especially strong when the social group with which we share our intentions is one with which we strongly identify, such as fellow workers in your profession, or fellow artists[78]. You can therefore leverage the motivational benefits of this strategy by working together with a group of peers in your field. Among other things, they will have a better understanding of what your plans will involve, and the struggles required to achieve them. A great example of this in action is National Novel Writing Month (or "NaNoWriMo"), a worldwide programme in which writers commit to writing a novel of at least 50,000 words during a single month (it runs in November each year), and post their daily word counts on the NaNoWriMo website for all to see. They can also form subgroups with their own direct contacts.

With all such commitments, the more public the better,

although it is worth noting that how motivated we are by the judgement of others may depend partly on personality. Author and podcaster Gretchen Rubin has outlined a framework of four 'tendencies', where people are categorised as obliger, questioner, upholder or rebel[79]. An *obliger* tendency is strongly motivated by others, more even than by their own preferences. A *questioner* type is less likely to be driven by external expectations as they like to ask things like, "why do we need to do this? Does this rule even make sense?" However, questioners do stick to their own internal set of rules and morals. *Upholders* have a strong drive to follow both internal and external rules. Finally a *rebel* tendency is less motivated by either their own expectations or those of others but they can be motivated by aspects of their identity that they value, for example their art. While there is still a lack of supporting evidence for Rubin's framework, it is certainly worth noting that if you see yourself as an upholder or obliger, you are likely to benefit more from making public commitments than if you identify as a questioner or rebel.

Another useful prompt as you are building a new habit is to set reminders. As noted above, new habits don't develop straight away – there will come a time when something really is habitual, but up until that point you will need to use strategies to help to maintain it. This can be compared to the little reminders that a driving instructor gives when you are learning to drive ('check your mirrors', 'indicate' and so on), which gradually decrease in frequency as these basic skills become automatic. With your creative habits, such reminders are not going to come from others (at least, not outside of lessons/classes that you take), but you could set them up for yourself. For example, try setting a recurring reminder via your phone or voice assistant at a time when you have decided to fit in an hour of creative work, avoiding the possibility that you forget about it until it's too late.

Again, working with an existing framework will help a lot – perhaps you have a clear hour between eating and clearing up your evening meal and putting the kids to bed, or a time after the daily dog walk which you typically spend playing games on your phone? The associations with the existing routines will, over time, come to act as a prompt, makes it much less likely that the new habit-in-the-making will be forgotten, and making the digital reminder cease to be necessary after a few weeks.

A good area to find some regular time is within the morning routine. For most people, there are a fairly predictable set of actions which they carry out in the morning, regardless of what variety the rest of the day holds. As such, this is a good time to slot in a regular habit. Even without trying for an uncomfortably early rise, perhaps you can block out 20-30 minutes for planning, brainstorming, writing or sketching (see also **Strategy 9** on why the time just after waking is very suitable for creative work).

Doing anything new with your time means, in some sense, giving up something else. After all, you haven't increased the number of hours in the day. If you want to spend an extra two hours a day practicing and composing music, what's going to give? It will be a lot easier if you can identify a specific task to cut out, and a specific time of day at which this currently occurs (again, because this involves fitting the new habit within an existing routine). A good example might be if you spend an hour a day watching TV news in the evening. This time could be directly swapped over to your creative project instead (the diary log from **Strategy 12** could be helpful here, if you are unaware where your time goes!).

Perhaps there are certain times of day that you spend scrolling through social media, which could be swapped for planning or editing of your work. Again, it's best if you know your own limits and make realistic commitments that you are likely to stick with - don't try to get rid of all of your leisure down time.

It's always going to be hard to give up things that we are used to, but there may be some time-consuming routines that don't actually add much to your life. Did you know, for example, that it can make people less happy to spend the time reading the news[80], or using Facebook[81]? Perhaps there is a more efficient way of staying informed, such as getting a daily news email or listening to a podcast with the key headlines, particularly if you can do this during a time when you could not realistically be doing productive creative work, for example when standing on a busy bus. Condensing these tasks into a single, focused session will be more time efficient than letting them bleed into multiple periods of the day, and doing so will also help you carve out times for your new routines.

Key tips:

- Creative work is easier if you get into working habit, but be aware that these take a long time to fully establish. Be realistic about your aims, and provide yourself with rewards (and use nudge strategies) particularly at the start and during holidays.
- Habits are easier to build into existing routines, such as your working day, your commute, or around relatively fixed and habitual aspects of your home life.
- Make a public commitment, for example by joining a challenge or by sharing your aim and the progress towards

it on social media. For the best results, ensure that this commitment is shared with a group of people who share your creative interests.

Strategy 14: Find the Best Times of Day

"Our lives present a never-ending stream of 'when' decisions."
    Daniel Pink, science writer.[82]

A popular stereotype of the creative individual features someone working into the small hours over their latest masterpiece. However, many artists start early and work a roughly 9-5 schedule, treating the process like any other day job. Some even do all of their work before the standard working day has started; architect Frank Lloyd Wright did most of his creative work between 4-7 a.m., leaving many who knew him confused about when he got his work done because they never observed it (he also took a nap later in the day to catch up on sleep – see **Strategy 9**)[83].

Many writers have taken a similar approach, fitting in the bulk of their work before breakfast either through choice or necessity (poet Sylvia Plath did so because her sleeping pills wore off in the middle of the night). If it suits you, getting a good amount of work done early on – rather than having it hanging over you – has the potential to be highly motivating.

Of course, working time is a highly individual choice, and

depends on family and work circumstances. What the variation among successful creatives tells us is that there is not a particular right or wrong time to work. However, that doesn't mean that anyone could work well at any given time. In fact, people's body clocks vary, meaning that different individuals are more productive at different times of day.

You probably already have a view of whether you are a morning or an evening person (sometimes called 'larks' and 'night owls' respectively), but are you clear on when your most productive time is — when you do your very best work? The concept of people being either larks or night owls has scientific backing (it's technically called your *chronotype*), and appears to be largely genetic[84]. Our level of attention and focus, and consequently our ability to successfully engage in creative thinking, problem solving and metacognition, varies through the day. Even if you consider yourself to be entirely an evening person, levels of focus and attention still drop as the night draws on, making it harder to focus on new or complex tasks.

In **Strategy 9**, I described how the period immediately after sleep or after a nap can be a good time to do creative work. Interestingly, the rest of the day can likewise be divided up into better or worse times for creativity. As Daniel Pink discusses in his fascinating book *When — the scientific secrets of perfect timing*[85], most people are better at doing problem solving tasks and work which requires a lot of focus in the early to mid-morning — meaning that this is an excellent time for strategy work, analysis, editing, or tasks that require the completion of complex procedures. In the afternoon and evening, people tend to be poorer at those tasks — but at those times they become better at lateral thinking, forming connections, and idea generation. To put it simply, people have a creative time of day and an analytic time of day. And perhaps surprisingly, they are more creative at their less preferred time.

What's especially fascinating, though, is that the above pattern is reversed for the 25% or so of us who are genuine night owls, meaning that this quarter of the population are more creative in the morning, and better at focused problem solving in the evening. Both larks and owls tend to suffer from a slump in the middle of the day when they are at their worst, though it occurs a bit earlier for larks. If you are still unsure whether you are a lark or an owl, search online for the *Horne-Ostberg questionnaire*– there are many web-based versions, and all will give you a simple estimate of your chronotype based on your preferences and habits.

Having identified your chronotype, it may be possible for you to figure out when to attempt your more challenging creative work, and when to allocate time to more routine tasks. While there isn't a single good time of day for all creative work, it can be helpful to consider the different tasks that you need to accomplish as part of your broader creative process, and identify suitable times for each. This way, you will be working with your body's natural rhythms and cognitive limitations rather than against them. You can allocate tasks as follows:

- The time (morning or evening) that fits your chronotype preference: analytical tasks such as problem solving, editing, or new learning/reading.
- The time (morning or evening) that does not fit your chronotype preference (e.g. in the morning, if you are a night owl): creative tasks such as coming up with new ideas, brainstorming, making links.
- Middle of the day: routine and non-essential tasks for which neither analysis nor creativity are required e.g. clearing up

materials, responding to emails.

As an example, an academic who was writing a research article should devoted their more creative time of day to original analysis and composition of an argument or coming up with new research ideas, with the analytic time of day devoted to reading and summarising prior work, or to proofreading and re-writing (which require a lot of focus to avoid errors creeping in). The middle-day slump could be used for routine emails, running errands, or attending meetings.

As chronotype is so individually variable, it would be helpful to test out when you do your best work, and to see whether changes are proving beneficial. One way of approaching this would be to keep a note over a week or so of when you felt most tired or alert. You could also test yourself on simple and more complex tasks. If you want to be really scientific about this, you can find tasks online that will test abilities such as the speed of your reactions or basic cognitive functions such as short-term memory for a list of random words, and test yourself at various times of day over the course of at least a week.

There are also things that we can do to modify our own alertness to make the most of our non-optimal times of day, the most obvious of which are eating, drinking, taking naps (see **Strategy 9**) and consuming drugs. In the latter category, by far the most popular is caffeine (and I certainly don't advocate anything stronger). Researchers do not entirely agree upon whether caffeine improves attention well enough to really boost the creative process other than by keeping us awake or speeding up our recover from naps (see **Strategy 9**). It's worth noting that despite the popularity of drinking strong coffee in the morning, caffeine acts on the brain by blocking adenosine, a chemical that builds up during the day and is associated with the fatigue that we feel in the evening. Its 'impact' on sleepiness in the morning may therefore be largely a placebo, although it is a stimulant and can therefore boost a person's focus. Later in the day, you may want to bear in mind that it takes 5-6 hours for the level of the caffeine in the bloodstream to drop even by half, and so its effects can affect later sleep quality if consumed in the afternoon or beyond [86] (with possible knock-on effects on productivity the following morning).

My own experience of using caffeine to boost productivity is that I used to regularly fall asleep on my train from work home; a well-timed strong coffee in the mid-afternoon now means that I write or edit for the entire journey instead – in this case, it's not so much the caffeine itself, but the timing and how it is used that matters.

Key tips:

- Idea generation and the early stages of the creative processes can work well when you first wake up.
- Identify your best time for both creative and analytic work, and schedule tasks accordingly. This depends on your chronotype – if, like most people, you are a morning 'lark', then you would be best to work on analytical tasks in the morning and creative tasks in the evening. 'Night owls' have the reverse pattern.
- Make limited use of caffeine in the afternoon and evening, but try not to disrupt your night's sleep.

Strategy 15: Plans and Snowflakes

"Before I undertake a lengthy project, I have usually given much thought to it over a period of years. my files are filled with likely subjects – which perhaps, one day, I will develop."

Joyce Carol Oates, author.[87]

S o now you have found your best time to work, set yourself up an inspiring and comfortable work space with no distractions, and carved out time in parts of your day to begin establishing a good creative work habit. What about the actual project?

Every project needs a plan of some sort. Some people may tell you that they don't plan. They do. It's just that they don't write their plans down. This might sound impressive, but really it just gives them a sneaky 'out' – if they haven't told anyone what they planned to do, then nobody can criticise them for not doing it. In fact, these individuals may intuitively be avoiding the public commitment 'nudge' discussed earlier (see **Strategy 12**).

The process of planning connects to the set of psychological abilities known as *metacognition*, a term meaning 'thinking about thinking'. It includes multiple processes which are absolutely essential to the creative process, such as reflecting on your ideas, planning your creative work, and evaluating what you have produced. In short, it is the mental skill of controlling our own thoughts (see also **Strategy 16**).

In the case of a creative project, a key aspect of metacognition includes thinking about new creative ideas, something that may seem particularly difficult and counterintuitive – how can we think about ideas that we haven't had yet? Metacognition is particularly associated with the frontal lobe of the brain, and is slow to fully develop – these abilities don't stop improving until the brain has fully matured, which takes place at around our mid-20s. It is also dependent on time of day, and on mental focus – it is one of the focused analytic tasks discussed in the previous section. What this means is that it is best to plan (and to re-evaluate and edit a plan) when your mental focus is at a good level – perhaps even after a power nap (see **Strategy 9**).

Planning also helps with motivation (see **Strategy 11**); a good plan helps you to divide a complex piece of work in to manageable stages, and to work through them one at a time (and not necessarily in order from first to last – when you plan well, this shouldn't matter too much!). Throughout life, large projects are always divided up in ways that makes them easier to undertake. In schools, for example, a teacher wouldn't hand pupils an entire project to do or set of books to read and expect them to just get on with it. Instead, long and complex projects are broken into bite-sized pieces. As an adult creative, you need to do this for yourself.

The heading in this section refers to one way of doing this that originated in the field of creative writing. The *snowflake technique* is a method of planning out a piece of writing, whereby the key elements are initially written down as a single paragraph with perhaps four or five sentences. These are then expanded – drawing an analogy to a snowflake which has multiple branches (technically called 'dendrites'), each of which divide into further branches if viewed closely enough. So, from a one paragraph summary, the writer then expands into a one-page overview (each sentence now becoming a paragraph), then a four or five-page version which covers most of the major plots/subplots and characters. Finally these are expanded into the main sections of the work.

In his book *Into the woods: how stories work and why we tell them,* TV screenwriter John Yorke notes that all stories, from films to plays to epic novels, follow a basic five-act structure[88]. They tend to have a beginning with an 'inciting incident' where the protagonist first experiences a problem and/or feels the antagonist working against them, a three-part middle which includes a 'moment of truth' when the characters learn key information as well as a dramatic crisis where characters face their darkest moment, and then an ending where the story is resolved, for good or ill. Curiously, he adds that each individual scene has the same structure, with some kind of struggle and resolution. This may help to explain why the snowflake technique can be so helpful - stories, by their nature, have a fractal, snowflake-like structure.

While it is most widely used by novelists, the snowflake technique could be applied to any written medium, including short stories, scripts, articles, or non-fiction work. In visual media, storyboards or sketches could play a similar role, particularly when used as plans. Indeed, any technique where you begin with an overview and develop simple outlines into detailed work is following a similar principle. In some creative fields such as recording music, film making or computer game design, the planning/rough sketch stage may be done collaboratively, and the final delivery of each completed part of the work undertaken by different individuals.

When planning longer projects, a plan that divides a larger piece of work into stages and associated time periods can be highly motivating as it allows you to see what you have done in a particular session, and set specific and manageable targets. It can be applied to academic writing, business projects and the creation of art exhibits. Even a very lengthy project can be divided into dozens or hundreds of stages, with a clear sense of progress resulting from ticking off one or two of these stages per week. This doesn't mean to say that you are taking creativity out of the equation – each part in itself is a small creative work, for which you may decided to follow some of the strategies discussed earlier in this book.

It's helpful to divide each stage of your plan into smaller steps where possible. When you do so, and view the list of tasks and sub-tasks, it's easy to make the assumption that each are quite similar in length, but they probably won't be. Consider each task before it starts, refer to how long similar tasks took in the past, and always allow a little extra time. Ultimately, it's more motivating to tick off lots of short tasks and to do things more quickly than expected, so hack this motivation by dividing your tasks into many parts from the outset.

One thing that makes it difficult to set realistic goals and divided tasks up well is that humans are fundamentally quite bad at predicting how long a process will take. This is known as the *planning fallacy*, and is one of a number of biases in how people think about the world and about their own behaviour[89]. Roger Buehler and colleagues have conducted a number of experiments showing that people tend to greatly underestimate task time, even when they have experience of doing similar tasks in the past. In one such study, students were asked to make a realistic estimate of how long they thought they would take to write an assignment, and were also asked to make a further estimate, saying how long they thought it would take if everything went as badly as possible. When these estimates were compared with actual task times, fewer than 30% of participants had finished by their 'accurate' estimate, and even by the 'worst possible' estimate, only around half had actually completed the work[90].

While we are all subject to cognitive biases, knowing about the planning fallacy indicates that we should allow much more time for each stage of a project than we would expect to be required. Doing so makes us more likely to stick to the plan, reduces stress, and saves time that would otherwise be needed for rescheduling at a later point. It will be helpful to keep notes and reflect on how long you actually spent on each part of a project, so you have written evidence to improve your planning in the future. However, do not fall into planning-fallacy trap of saying to yourself, "that took 5 hours last time because of x, but I'll do it much quicker this time round".

Make sure that the time to do a task is listed on your to-do list, alongside the task itself. If you do finish a task early, take the remaining time to have a short break, go for a coffee or make a non-essential phone call, rather than going straight on to the next task. Doing so builds in a reward for your hard work and efficiency, and also encourages you to make accurate (rather than unrealistically short) time estimates for future tasks. It's also healthier, helping you to defuse the level of mental tension which will have built up as you worked on the task.

Key tips:

- Plan and evaluate your own planning during a time of day when you are focused and alert, as it requires complex metacognition.
- When planning, begin with an overview, and then move to gradually greater levels of detail – the snowflake method or similar outlining techniques can work very well for this.
- Break large tasks into smaller steps. Remember the planning fallacy bias of underestimating the time required, and use past experience to inform future time allocation.

Strategy 16: From Draft to Finished Product

"I have exploded many baked potatoes in my time. Some-times I have opened the oven door to find that just the skins remain, while the flesh has pebble-dashed the inside of my oven."
  Nigel Slater, chef and writer.[91]

There is some debate over how much great the creative geniuses of the past drafted and edited their work. Historically, it was often assumed that Mozart produced his work more or less fully formed, in one mighty creative outpouring. However, modern scholars (as well as documentary evidence) suggest that each of his compositions moved through several stages, from early sketches to fuller but still incomplete musical scores[92].

Overall, it's difficult to know whether the cases of individuals who have produced creative work without drafts or plans (or at least appeared to), are entirely what they seem. Scottish poet Norman McCaig, for example, claimed not to redraft his work at all – but then, a poem is short enough to have been largely composed (and effectively redrafted) mentally before setting it down on paper. In any case, such individuals are clearly the exception rather than the rule.

In contrast, many people refer with a certain pride to how much they re-work early versions of their creative works. Many authors are frank about the limitations of their first drafts, seeing this as a normal – indeed, indispensable – part of the process. The idea that 'books aren't written, they're re-written' is an adage among creative writers.

Most creative fields have some kind of re-working or editing stage as part of the overall process. In the case of computer coding, this might involve debugging, while in fields such as architecture and science, there might be a formal method for gaining peer or client feedback on early versions. Other endeavours lend themselves to multiple practice attempts before a final performance, such as early sketches that lead to a final work, musical recordings, or giving a workplace presentation. These, too, benefit from a process of feedback and gradual improvement. Even in fields which lend themselves more to a one-off production – stand-up comedy, for example – there is a lengthy process of preparation, practice and working on material that goes on before the final product, with a great deal of thinking and reflection.

On a practical level, you will need to develop an effective set of routines and practices for moving your work from a draft or practice stage to the finished product. Once a 'first draft' copy of your work (sketch, recording, script, etc) is complete, it is worthwhile changing the format of this in order to view it more as an audience would, for example by switching from the computer screen to physical materials, such as a recording or printout. This makes psychological sense – seeing material presented differently makes it less likely that the brain will rely on memory, making it easier to focus on details and to spot flaws. For written work, it would make sense to print a draft in a different size and font in order to boost this benefit. Photographers may gain the same benefit by viewing their work in a different physical location or from different perspectives and under different lighting. Even TV or video materials could be viewed in full from a different distance and on a different-sized screen.

Editing and refining your work will no doubt feel like a chore at times, but trimming out excess material and selecting among different options can greatly improve the quality of the end product. Another famous saying, attributed to several writers including T. S. Eliot and Mark Twain, is: "if I'd had more time, I'd have written a shorter letter". It may even become enjoyable after the more difficult decisions are out of the way. It is good practice to keep everything that you cut or take out, just in case – an idea, sequence or image cut because it didn't fit well in a previous work could end up providing the seed of a future one. They are, after all, your ideas; keep them, value them, return to them (after a suitable period of time – see **Strategy 10**!).

Similarly, it is important to record each step of the process in such a way that you can take another look at and perhaps return to an earlier stage if necessary. This applies most obviously to fields such as music and video recording, writing, or graphic design, but it could also apply to science, coding, and many other contexts. In some visual media or fields where discussion plays a key part of the process, it may be necessary to find some way of documenting this or taking snapshots. For creatives whose work is primarily computer-based, it should be straightforward to make frequent backups – it would be a shame to lose ideas and snippets that could prove useful in a future project. The next section discusses this further.

What to change and what to keep is perhaps the most difficult question for any creative professional. When you have nagging doubts, are they valid concerns or are you just being overly anxious and self-critical? Previous sections have discussed getting trusted feedback and finding ways of creating enough of a distance that we can look at our own work with fresh eyes (see **Strategy 9**). Ultimately, though, there comes a point where you need to make the tough calls, 'kill your darlings', and implement crucial changes to your work in progress.

In the early stages of a creative career, people tend to have well-developed critical faculties, but a less well advanced set of creative skills – as TV and radio producer Ira Glass memorably described it, there tends to be a *taste gap* whereby the artist's creative taste is more refined than their fledgling skills[93].

This makes sense on a psychological level, because both of these things are in large part a matter of practice and developed expertise. We know from many areas of psychology that experts think differently from novices – they remember more and learn more rapidly in their area of expertise, are better at sifting relevant from irrelevant details, and can make good judgements almost automatically[94]. At the outset, every creative is a much more expert critic than they are a practitioner, due to having been consuming and criticising other people's work for years. No wonder there is a tendency to have self-doubts.

During these stages, it is important to recognise that early attempts are valuable – they may not be ready for public consumption, but you will have learned a lot from doing them. Learning from others' work and creating your own is an *iterative process* – a cycle, but one that continually moves forward, with each stage providing feedback that develops the next. In other words, creating makes you a better and more insightful critic of your own work, and also better able to perceive how other artists or writers have handled and overcome difficulties. And as you perceive this more, it feeds into your own work. As a new photographer, for example, you no longer just see what looks like a 'nice photograph', but you start to observe the lighting and aperture used, and intuitively understand the artistic choices that cause the piece to be effective. Such ideas can then be taken back to enrich your own future work.

British fantasy author David Eddings is of the opinion that authors need to write at least a million words of basic-quality material before really hitting your stride, preferably throwing the previous work away. "*At that point*", he says, "*you're ready to begin*"[95]. This compares interestingly with what researcher Anders Ericsson, in his work on expertise, has concluded – that people need 10,000 hours of practice. Indeed, Eddings may have underestimated the level of practice required, because a million words for that length of time equates to fewer than two words per minute. On the other hand, writers do not start off as complete beginners – they already have many hundreds of hours of practice from their school days and beyond. In other creative fields, this apprenticeship may take place throughout school, college and beyond, and could include several years of creative efforts and feedback in the workplace as a kind of creative apprenticeship.

It's worth noting that Ericsson and other psychologists view expert skill largely in terms of practice, rather than reflecting innate ability or potential. However, an important point about his theory – which has been applied not just to creative fields but also to professions such as surgery and teaching, and to sporting skill – is that this has to be *deliberate practice*, and can't be mindless or routine. For example, you wouldn't become an expert driver (to rival Formula 1 levels of skill, for example) by driving to work and back every day while daydreaming. Instead, you would maintain the same level of ability and continue to make the same errors. That kind of practice may actually make you worse at a task, as errors become gradually more automatic over time.

Deliberate practice has well defined characteristics: it involves focusing your full attention, it is directed at improving a specific skill, and it engages with a process of gaining timely, detailed feedback. In the example of an Olympic athlete, for example, they would receive feedback from a knowledgeable coach after each race or performance, focusing on specific details of their movements or timing. Do you get this level of feedback on your performance? Without it, practice is much less effective.

At a certain point, therefore, this means that to improve, you need seek out and act on feedback on your works in progress. It would be worth giving this some idea some thought, alongside trying to develop a growth mindset (see **Strategy 11**) when it comes to your own creative work, whereby criticism is seen as valuable rather than a threat, and skill as being fundamentally a matter of practice rather than talent. Nobody has ever reached a top level of achievement without challenging themselves. As Ken Robinson has argued, if you're not prepared to be wrong, you'll never come up with anything original [96]. So rather than sticking to things that are sure you can do well, challenge yourself – and value any mistakes as signs of progress.

In *The Road Less Travelled,* author and psychologist M Scott Peck discusses how most people tend towards one extreme or the other in their relationship with the world at large – 'neurotic' personalities tend to blame and doubt themselves excessively, while 'personality disordered' individuals tend to blame and doubt others[97]. Both approaches are problematic, and instead Peck advises us to take a middle road, where we recognise our own flaws but also have sufficient self-belief to keep going when others doubt us. Editing our own creative output and ideas can be seen in much the same way. When evaluating your own work, you need to be critical enough to make changes (unlike the stereotypical overconfident beginner who thinks that everyone else is just too short-sighted to recognise his genius), but not so self-critical that we throw our arms up in despair and give up, or make changes far beyond what was actually necessary. From this point of view, both the creative work and the creative person him/herself can benefit from moving from draft to finished product.

Key tips:

- Assume that successful creative work requires a process of preparation, drafting and re-drafting. This is nothing to be ashamed of!
- Keep hold of earlier versions or sections that were cut from a project, as they could be helpful later on.
- Expertise is a process of practice, but to be successful it needs to be focused, deliberate practice, where specific feedback is obtained.

Strategy 17: Recycling and Recombining

"I'm constantly experimenting, trying different ways of creating pieces and figuring out what works best."
    Kumi Yamashita, visual artist.[98]

F ollowing on from a point in the previous section, bits and pieces of previous projects can and should be cut where they don't fit or add to the final work, but they shouldn't be too rapidly discarded. There are various ways to keep them – some keep a record of everything in notebooks, some file things neatly in binders or as digital files, while others have more of a jumble of 'old work' that they would rather not look through.

If you're really not sure what to do with a set of ideas, perhaps you should let random chance take control? Following on from the ideas of the Dada movement in poetry and art (see **Strategy 3**), one approach to this would be to decide which items to focus on by rolling dice or using a computer to generate a set of random numbers. The numbered items can then be looked at together, after which you can pursue any connections that suggest themselves. Although bringing in this much chaos into the process won't suit everyone, it's worth bearing in mind – as discussed in Part 1 – how hard it can be to break out of the habits of thoughts and associations that we have learned and automated over the years. Another, similar option would be to have a try at putting some of the part-completed ideas, characters, paragraphs, musical phrases, scenes or plot lines onto index cards, shuffling them, then spreading them out across a desk to see what might go with what. And then do it again.

There is a research basis to the idea of bringing more randomness into the creative process. In a 2017 paper entitled *Ideas rise from chaos,* Yeun Joon Kim and Chen-Bo Zhong of the University of Toronto argue that a set of items that are not easily categorised can stimulate more creative thinking than an orderly set. Referring back to the work of Guilford, they suggest that organisation, while useful on one level, tends to lead items in a set to be interpreted in terms of the first item seen – for example, these are all types of animals: dog, cat, mouse, elephant, sloth. A more random set (such as pudding, Ukraine, check, mouse, and symphony), does not suffer from that problem[99]. This can lead to your mind seeking out order and meaning from the set of items. As such connections are meaningfully distant, the items prompt a form of creative problem solving (see also **Strategy 3**).

When I first started writing, I began a file called "One good idea", in which I put any little phrase, scene or concept that I thought could make its way into a later story. Over time, as I became more focused on writing non-fiction books, this was joined by files on "Research ideas", "Possible book titles" and so forth. I will no doubt only use a fraction of them, but reading back through such snippets is a useful task for getting out of a creative rut. So hold on to your half-formed ideas and plans.

Even if you never use them, it's a lot better than discarding an idea that could have been helpful.

Of course, while it's great to note down images and half-formed ideas, it's also vital to learn how to craft a set of ideas into a bigger work. This is where experience comes in, and a synergy between consuming and producing creative work (see **Strategy 16**). Psychologically, this reflects the difference between an individual concept or memory and a broader structure. A *schema* is a mental model of a concept (e.g. a house, a meal, a conversation or a workshop), including not just what it is, but also what it is used for. It is a generic and adaptable structure of mental associations, unique to each individual and developed throughout our lives[100]. Most memory researchers believe that all of our knowledge is structured into these schemas. This means that to work effectively, the things that we know must be interconnected, with each specific memory linked to a more generic understanding of how the world works.

In the case of a creative idea, for example a character that will appear in a film or a book, this is not much to go on by itself, but when combined with a context it can be very powerful. In his book *The Anatomy of Story*, screenwriter John Truby explains that the protagonist of a story should be developed in tandem with the character or set of characters that will attempt to stop them attaining their goals[101]. In a similar way, creative works such as a film, art exhibition or architectural designs, or even a recipe, all depend not just on individual elements but on the synthesis that makes up the whole.

As mentioned before, it can be useful to keep hold of incomplete pieces of work. It is also worthwhile to review these separately, away from the main body of work; we know that seeing things out of context can make it harder to remember, and can also help to prompt creative ideas (see **Strategy 6**). Doing so could prompt an accidental juxtaposition of ideas that stimulates a new idea, or could take off into a completely new work of its own. You can also choose to subject each part-complete works to the systematic methods of idea generation discussed earlier in this book, such as mind mapping or brain-storming (see **Strategies 1 and 3**).

Key tips:

- Keep careful track of your creative ideas, filing items in ways that make them easy to access periodically – it can take a long time before you find the right context to use a particular idea.
- Look for links between these snippets of ideas that you have recorded – the more varied, the better. Try out unusual or random mixtures from time to time of older ideas, looking for ways that a single element could fit into the broader framework of a creative project.
- Reconsider and develop part-complete ideas away from their original context, trying out some of the idea generation techniques that you have learned in order to take them in a different direction.

Strategy 18: Pressure Yourself - But Not Too Much

"Man should not try to avoid stress any more than he would shun food, love or exercise."
    Hans Selye, scientist.[102]

Stress is a bad thing, of course...? Not always. Yes, stress can be harmful to the body and make you more prone to illness[103], and it's also harmful to productivity to be overstimulated. However, according to the long-established *Yerkes-Dodson* law, it can also be problematic if you are not stimulated enough[104]. Instead, the ideal point for your creative work will be to aim for a midpoint.

Imagine, for example, an athlete – without a cheering crowd they don't strain quite as hard to win, but in a gold-medal race the pressure may be too much, becoming counterproductive. In other words, therefore, a bit of pressure can be a good thing. To quote from Douglas Adams' classic sci-fi novel *The Hitchhiker's Guide to the Galaxy*, there's "*nothing more useless than a bored archaeologist*"[105].

The key idea here is that there is a sweet spot in terms of performance where you are motivated, feeling a little bit of pressure, but not overwhelmed. This may not be easy to achieve, but it's important to aim for. Being too stressed in creative projects may be down to deadlines and other external pressures, and the main way to manage this is via planning (see **Strategy 15**).

Not being stressed enough may seem like an odd concept in an era when the World Health Organisation has declared workplace stress and related mental health to be a problem of epidemic proportion[106]. To understand this, imagine how you feel several hours prior to a deadline for a project. Compare the workload several months in advance, at the beginning of that period, to how things play out towards the end. Being under-stressed can lead to poor prioritising and a false sense of security – or just simple procrastination. But of course, the final moments can be far too intense.

Many creative professionals are well aware of the power of a deadline, but do little to use this in their favour. An optimal level of stress can improve output and creative thinking by applying just the right amount of pressure in a way that is ongoing, rather than via a last-minute panic. In the NaNoWriMo challenge (discussed in **Strategy 13**), writers, often very inexperienced ones, write a novel of 50,000 words or more in a month. Most achieve this by breaking it down into several challenging but achievable goals, essentially aiming for an average of 1667 words per day. This is a tough challenge but many writers can do it (over 25% 'win' by uploading a manuscript of over 50k words[107]). The benefit of such challenges lie in maintaining the pressure at a relatively constant level, in effect hacking the experience of pressure to increase productivity in the early stages, and attenuating it later on.

Of course repeated short-term challenges such as daily deadlines may be too relentless to be sustainable over the long haul, and so it is worth thinking of other ways to maintain sensible levels of pressure and avoid slacking. The benefits of making a public commitment have already been discussed (see **Strategy 12**), and even without doing this, having external scrutiny of your progress can provide a necessary boost to motivation. Again, there is the potential to hack this situation by promising to deliver a project piece by piece, rather than having a single huge deadline. Sensible PhD advisors are well aware of this, asking for work to be submitted section by section, rather than setting a single deadline for a 100,000-word thesis at the end of three years!

The effects of stress is now known to be more than just a matter of quantity, however. Canadian-Hungarian researcher Hans Selye is credited with developing our modern concept of stress, based on his work as a doctor in the 1930s. One of the key insights he presented in his early work was that stress leads to a general physical reaction – the same set of symptoms, regardless of the stressor. However in his 1974 book *Stress Without Distress* he moved away from this view, recognising that in some situations, stress can be positive. He began to distinguish between *eustress* (good stress) and *distress* (bad stress)[108]. Distress, he argues, doesn't lead to any positive outcome, and is likely to make you give up or avoid tasks, while eustress can be motivating, and even though it has unpleasant aspects, it generally feels positive (think about the feelings of achievement associated with completing a productive day of work on a valuable a large project, or with meeting one of the part-deadlines discussed above).

The distinction between whether than event is experienced as distress or eustress is largely psychological – it depends upon how we think about and react to it. Do we feel in control? Does the stress link to our aims and to aspects of our identity the we value, and form a part of a clear larger goal? Or, on the other hand, is it just part of the daily grind, not getting you anywhere? The cumulative effects of such small-scale hassles are linked to ill-health[109], while the pressure that links to your meaningful broader goals and which you feel is under control is much more tolerable.

Stress can also be modified and managed by a variety of coping techniques, some of which are much more helpful than others. What psychologists call *emotion-focused coping* involves making ourselves feel better in various ways, tackling the stress in the short term but not doing anything about its source. Examples might include denial of our problems, snapping at co-workers, moaning to friends, going back to bed and trying not to think about it, or even substance use. On the other hand, *problem-focused coping* involves reacting to stress by using strategies that tackle the source of the problem, for example making a to-do list or asking experienced friends for advice on how they overcame similar problems. Looking at this objectively, it should be clear that emotion-focused coping is a short-term fix, and that the problems are likely to get worse, not better! The way that we react to stress is not an inevitable part of our character, and we can choose problem-focused coping strategies that will break down and tackle the source of the stress.

One of the most useful problem-focused ways of managing our stress is through time management and prioritisation. Writing to-do lists is one simple strategy which can be applied to nearly any creative field. A helpful way to enhance the basic to-do list is known as the *ABC technique*. This involves labelling each task 'A', 'B' or 'C' according to importance – the As are urgent and important, the Bs are not urgent but still important, while the Cs are nice to have, but neither urgent nor important. You then work through the As first, then the Bs, and leave Cs for any remaining time. The main aim of this is to limit the risk of missing key deadlines, while ensuring that some fun tasks are still included (but these don't get done first, which would result in procrastination).

This management of stress in your life can be applied more broadly, not just in creative projects, and it may well make sense to implement a combined to-do list of both household tasks and your work, as keeping them all in one place will make it easier to keep track of (rather than managing several to-do lists). Anything that has not been completed can simply be promoted to the start of the next day's list. Just make sure that the former are not always prioritised as 'B' or 'C' – it's all too easy to let creative projects slide altogether when dealing with relentless family or career demands. As described in previous sections, carve out time to work on them by identifying regular times in your schedule, and work through the nice, short items in your to-do list at a rate of at least one per day. This way, you'll get the sense of life goal-relevant progress which is very motivating over the long term. Challenge and pressure yourself – but not too much!

Key tips:

- Manage stress by finding ways of spreading it out over time, such as having staged deadlines rather than one big deadline at the end of a project.
- Recognise that stress can be beneficial when it links to life goals, and tackle harmful stress via problem-focused coping

methods.

· Identify aims as A, B or C in order of priority and urgency, tackling the As first and making use of a to-do list.

Strategy 19: The Long Haul

"When disruption leads to great success, the world is pacified. It is beneficial to cross great rivers, in the sense that there is purpose in your actions. Three days before and three days after refer to creative action, which begins again after it finishes."
    The I Ching.[110]

I f we want to work productively over the long term, we need to think beyond daily tasks or techniques, or even individual routines. Creativity, like many things in life, is more likely to reward the long-distance runner than the sprinter, and the cumulative effect of working effectively for longer – five hours instead of three per day, for example – could be huge. This section considers the psychology of long working sessions.

According to mainstream psychology and neuroscience, everything that we think and do has its roots in the brain. This needn't concern you overly – after all, people were working in all of the major creative fields long before this was understood (the great philosophers of Ancient Greece didn't even know that thinking was done by the brain!). However, the functions and limitations of the human brain are worth understanding if you are to get the best out of yours. Taking into account the basic biology of the brain and body, there is no doubt that despite high motivation and a few doses of caffeine, people can't keep working at a high level indefinitely.

The human brain is made up of billions of neurons, and these form interconnected brain structures which each have different functions. The brain is also a dynamic organ, subtly changing in structure as we learn and on the basis of experience[111]. Linking back to what was discussed under **Strategy 7**, there is a great deal of processing that goes on in the brain without our conscious awareness, from visual processing to the automatic recall of memories. Many of these processes even happen while we are asleep.

A mind at work requires a steady supply of its basic physiological fuel. Immediately after sleep we may feel sluggish, and we are at our best at certain parts of the day, the details of which depend on our chronotype (see **Strategy 14**). At all times, the brain requires energy in the form of glucose, as well as water and nutrients. Some chemicals are replenished in brain cells when we are sleeping, making sleep a physiological necessity, too. As long as we are not deprived from those essentials, we will be able to function. Stimulants such as caffeine and nicotine can boost functioning, but their effects tend to be quite short-term, and we also develop a tolerance to such drugs. Depressant drugs such as alcohol reduce our attention and focus.

The conscious part of the mind depends primarily on the frontal lobe of the cerebral cortex – the area behind your forehead and between the temples. It is responsible for working memory, the part of immediate thinking and processing that deals with small amounts of information in the here-and-now – in other words, whatever's in your mind at a particular moment. It also integrates logical and emotional processing, and is essential for metacognition – helping us to think about our own thinking, and to monitor our own performance.

Supplying the brain's basic needs underlies our ability to concentrate. We have probably all experienced feeling that we just can't focus due to being fatigued or hungry. While it's an educational myth that nobody can concentrate on a lecture for more than ten minutes[112], it's also true that concentration tends to drop in the second half of an hour's lecture or lesson[113]. This, of course, is a passive task, and active tasks such as creating our own work are much easier to maintain focus on, especially if we achieve a flow state.

Varying your working practices such that you are engaging in a mixture of different tasks will help when it comes to maintaining attention levels. Numerous research studies have shown that attention naturally tends to drop when items or tasks are repeated. Variety is the spice of life, and also the food of cognitive processes. Your attention levels will be more easily maintained if you can structure a working day such that you are switching from one type of task to another (perhaps working on a new project in the morning and reviewing and improving an existing work in the afternoon).

Did you ever, when reading a book or writing an essay during your school days, find your mind drifting on to other things? Attention is essential for new learning, and daydreaming (or *mindwandering*, as cognitive psychologists call it) is therefore undoubtedly harmful for taking in new information or instructions – which is why the teacher would no doubt tell you to 'pay attention'. It's also true that when mindwandering, you are not directly progressing with the task at hand.

Curiously, however, mindwandering may have its benefits to creativity. An international team of psychologists led by Benjamin Baird of the University of California conducted a study where participants were asked to do a version of the Guilford alternative uses test (see **Strategy 1**). They were particularly interested in what happened during an incubation period, in between a first attempt at the task and a later task (which consisted of both new items and repetitions of the same items). In between, participants were divided among four situations, three of which lasted for twelve minutes: one group were given a demanding working memory task which took up all of their attention, one group was given a much less demanding task that was thought to promote mindwandering, and a third group simply had a break. The fourth group were given no additional task, and did the alternative uses task again immediately.

Findings showed that the undemanding task – which consisted of clicking to say whether numbers on the screen were odd or even – led to significantly improved performance on the creativity test, in terms of coming up with unusual uses for objects. Performance on the demanding task and rest conditions stayed about the same, while those who experienced the 'no break' conditions got worse. This supported the researchers' hypothesis that mindwandering plays a key role in incubation (see also **Strategies 6 & 10**), in particular because the benefit was only found with repeated items, not with new ones. Another important part of the findings is that participants in the undemanding condition didn't report thinking about the initial task any more than the other groups did – so the benefits of mindwandering were happening without focusing on the specific problem at hand[114].

Mindwandering can be seen as a useful counterpart to the

intense focus on a problem that occurs during brainstorming. It speaks against the use of long sessions of creative work – not only is it good to take a break to boost attention levels, but those breaks may result in helpful creative processing.

The mindwandering research also fits with evidence that retrieving information from memory such as when writing or conversing can be to the detriment of other information. In other words, recalling and focusing on something can make it more likely you'll forget something else. However, this can be a good thing. The benefits of a break or a period of mind-wandering may involve reducing the temporary mental fixation on a particular idea, giving other ideas a chance to come to mind. What's more, the 'forgotten' information is more easily learned at a later point, showing that it is only temporarily lost to the mind[115].

Given that a short break can potentially lead to useful mind-wandering and incubation, when exactly should we take them? The timing of breaks is actually very important, and plays a key role in a worker's ability to concentrate over a long session. From an analytical point of view, an important question is how best to time these breaks such that they are as effective as possible, but do not use up too much of our time. In other words, what is the optimal balance between break time and working time?

One possible answer to this question is the *pomodoro technique.* This is a method of time management that encourages us to focus for 25-minute spells, each followed by a shorter break of five minutes or so. Suitable break activities could include going for a short walk outside, getting yourself a drink, doing some exercise, or going to the toilet.

Pomodoro means 'tomato'; the technique is the creation of

Francesco Cirillo who initially used a tomato-shaped kitchen timer to time his 25-minute work periods. He explains that the action of twisting the timer and the mechanical 'clicks' as it slowly revolves are helpful to boost focus[116]. After four such 'pomodoros', you are advised to take a longer break of 20-30 mins, allowing for that essential refuelling.

The choice of a 25-minute session may seem rather arbitrary, and in practice, the optimal duration is likely to depend both on you as an individual and on the nature of the task. Each of us has a different attention span, and if you are absorbed and in a flow state, there is no reason to interrupt your work so frequently. This aspect therefore needs to be modified depending on your creative pursuit.

However, provided that it does not interrupt your train of thought, a sequence of short breaks is a good idea. This length of break is enough to give your eyes and mind a rest, but avoids a lengthy delay that could cause you to lose track of what you are doing (and perhaps leave the flow state), or get side-tracked by other projects.

You can download apps specifically aimed at the pomodoro technique, some of which are free. However, rather than setting a 25-minute timer followed by a shorter one, it is easier in practice to set a half-hour timer and then repeat. That way, the first few minutes after the timer goes off become your break (toilet break, short exercise, etc) and you return to the creative task straight after. This is even more efficient, and avoids the need to mess around with multiple timers.

Concentration over long stretches of time does depend partly on strategy, and it is possible to pace yourself and to force yourself to stay on task for longer, particularly if you choose to focus on specific things. Nevertheless, it's probably the case that lengthy work sessions are a poor use of time. When working late into the evening our judgement is likely to suffer, and the quality of work is likely to drop sharply. All-nighters, in particular, will lead to poor work and a loss of valuable sleep. It would be better in most cases – even where an essential deadline is looming – to nap for a few hours at least.

Key tips:

- The brain has basic physiological needs including glucose, water and sleep, so ensure that you are well rested, eating and drinking regularly.
- Mindwandering means that you are losing your ability to focus, but be aware of its potential benefits, too. This doesn't require you to intentionally think about a problem during breaks – indeed, doing so may be counterproductive.
- Build in multiple short breaks and an occasional longer break. These can break up 'pomodoro' working sessions, but be flexible – don't interrupt productive sessions to frequently if you are getting into a flow state.

Strategy 20: The Drive to Finalise

*"I've tried to write poetry and prose at the same time...
and it just doesn't work. I think they're two different
mindsets"*
   Simon Armitage, writer.[117]

R obert Sternberg's triarchic theory (discussed in **Strategy 3**) recognises that successful intelligence is not just a matter of problem solving, but also depends on our ability to put our intelligence into action. One person may have better cognitive skills, he argues, but another may be better at the 'street smarts' of tackling real-world situations.

The same can be said for creativity. Many highly creative people are not especially successful. Why not? In part, this rests on the skills of selecting among possible projects, and seeing them through to a productive conclusion. In this section we will focus on the skills that facilitate prolific and successful output.

As discussed throughout this book, creativity is not about the flashes of inspiration experienced by a few geniuses or brought to us by whimsical muses, but about learning the craft of forming and developing good ideas, and finding ways to develop these over the long term. Something creative needs to be not just original but also useful. It is therefore important both for success and time efficiency that we are able to prioritise among multiple ongoing projects.

Prioritising draws on our metacognitive abilities – we need to be able to reflect on what we have done, select among our ideas and improve on those which are most worthwhile of our time (see **Strategy 15**). Just as when observing new combinations we need to spot the more promising ones among the more mediocre. In part, this depends on the context in which you are working. Take a few minutes to consider the following questions for any ongoing or potential projects that you are currently considering:

1. If I complete this project, how much is it going to enhance the body of work that I have already done? Is it just more of the same?
2. How much time will it take to work on this project through to completion?
3. What career opportunities or financial rewards could come from completing this project, and how likely are they to occur?
4. What are the chances that I will actually finish this project at all, and if there are reasons why I might not, are they under my control?

As can be seen from the questions, we can take a long, hard, dispassionate look at each of the projects that could lie ahead of us. In some cases, something is worth investment and sacrifice because it involves creating something new, unique and valuable. In other cases, it might be just another project, very much like the ones we have done before. And we also need to consider the *opportunity cost* – any one project that we work on is taking time away from others which we could be completing instead. If we are to make the best use of our creative working time, we need the ability to recognise which promising ideas have genuine potential, and which will be more of a time sink.

Of course, some projects are much more time consuming than others. It can be motivating to get a quick win rather than tackling an enormous project from the outset. A creative writer, for example, might want to publish a couple of unrelated short stories before taking on a sequence of novel-length books. Those early works allow a honing of the necessary skills and provide opportunities for feedback, and can also help to build an audience who are interested in your work, and whose demands for more can add (extrinsic) motivation to continue. In other words, the opportunity cost of those short stories is low, and the potential rewards are great.

Bearing in mind the earlier discussion of process and drafting (see **Strategy 16**), you may also want to consider having two or more projects on the go. Again, this is partly a matter of motivation – when stuck on one area, it's probably a good time to move onto another. During this away time from the first project, if you are fortunate, some incubation of ideas may occur, perhaps during a period of mindwandering. Indeed, if your process is very refined, you may have multiple projects in the pipeline, all at different stages. Perhaps it will look something like this:

- A. A large set of early ideas, ready for combination into single projects
- B. A small set of 'ready to go' projects that are well thought-

out and planned in detail, but not actually started.

- C. One project where you are working towards a first version/first draft.
- D. One project where your first version is complete, and you are leaving it for a period of time, such that you will return to it with fresh eyes.
- E. One project which you are now returning to and re-working in order to take it from first version to completion.
- F. One or more projects which are largely complete, but which you are sending to peers for feedback and/or working on final edits.

From the above list, A and B are where you focus the planning and idea generation skills discussed in Part 1 of this book, while C and E are the projects that will be consuming most of your day-to-day working time. Alternating between these two projects may help to boost attention levels, as discussed in the previous section (and can also be done in a way that fits best with your chronotype – see **Section 14**).

Comparing all of the different projects at their different stages can help us to take a broader perspective – as well as thinking about the work, we can also think about our own processes, and consider such aspects as which we enjoyed more, and which was more successful. You may be able to look at the list above and identify areas where you are strong (for example, perhaps you are really good at getting a first draft down), and others where you need to improve (for example, perhaps you are poor at reaching that final completion stage, or at finding suitable ways of getting peer feedback).

In terms of the planning stage B, it's difficult to judge exactly how many projects anyone should be planning at a particular time. Too many, and you could end up spreading your ideas too thinly. Don't hold a great and relevant idea back, thinking that it's so good it deserves its own separate project. If it fits, use it. After all, the best creative projects have multiple interesting things going on. And you will have plenty more good ideas in the future.

There may also be a procrastination element to plans – some people regularly give in to the temptation to continually start planning something new exciting, but rarely take these forward to a complete work! From that point of view, take the processing of planning a new project seriously, and ask yourself some searching questions at the outset about whether you are really willing to spend at least a couple of days per week working on this. If not, it may not be worth putting time into planning it at all, at least at this stage in your career.

It might sound deeply counterproductive to make things more difficult for yourself by working on both a first draft and a 'later stage' project simultaneously, but having these different projects can allow you to switch when 'stuck', therefore staying motivated and being more time efficient overall. There can also be a cross-fertilisation of good ideas, if they are at least partly connected. Many creative ideas were in some sense borrowed or transferred across from a related domain, or involved a combination of more than one domain – Bob Dylan's fusion of rock and folk music in the 1960s, for example (see also **Strategy 7** on analogies). There can also be pragmatic benefits; if your projects are linked in some way – for example, two visual art projects for which you can use similar skills, form similar collaborations and perhaps use the same contacts when it comes to exhibitions or publications. Trying to learn very different sets of creative skills (e.g. architecture in the morning, musical composition in the afternoon) is not impossible, but it's definitely more demanding. Sadly it seems clear that practising our creative work doesn't make us better at creativity in general, but is largely domain specific[118].

It's also worth thinking about working with creative collaborators. To take an example from academia, some researchers in academia publish thousands of papers over their lifetime, and others only publish a few. This probably has less to do with ability, and more to do with finding good people to collaborate with, allowing each researcher's focus to be spent on the parts of the process to which they are best suited. For example, perhaps one member of a four-person team is good at coming up with early ideas and plans, one is good at drafting, one good at editing, and the final member is great at selling the work to agents, clients or other markets. Each team member is in a good place to drive forward with creative collaborations – in effect, they can each complete a different stage of the processes above, allowing each to produce much more than they would by themselves.

Over the long-term, successful creativity involves getting your work to its intended audience. When it comes to the finalisation stage (stage F, above), don't ignore the fact that this also takes a lot of time, not least because you will have to spend a lot of time waiting for other people. Unlike in early planning and drafting stages, your time is no longer your own when you are waiting for editors, galleries or peer feedback. This is why it is fine to have more than one project at this stage (although this may depend on your creative field). You can have dozens of brilliant works in progress in the pipeline, but this is not enough to ensure success.

Indeed, your productivity is as much a matter of strategy and well-utilised time as it is about how creative your brain is. Certain things are out of your control, but on the basis of having to be 'in it to win it', you can at least ensure that you are completing work at a reasonable rate, and sharing it with a suitable audience. This may involve setting particular opportunities as targets – a submission to a particular newspaper/journal/art competition that closes in three months' time, for example. Therefore you find yourself planning and structuring not just the steps of a project, but also your working life over the course of a year or so.

This planning is important when it comes to submissions, for example of articles to journals or scripts to TV channels, for most will not accept simultaneous submissions. Keep a careful note, ideally on a spreadsheet or table, of which items have been submitted, when, and to whom. Also take note of their response time, if available. Query any market (to use a broad term for any outlet that you submit creative work to) that has not responded within a month or so. The same applies to clients in the business world.

It's also a good idea to have a note of your second, third and fourth choice markets for this kind of submission, and for anything that is rejected, be ready to send the same work out to the next market on the list. Do your research here – many markets will only take particular types of work. If you are writing philosophical articles about education, don't submit it to a journal that only prints work based on quantitative data, as it will be immediately rejected and is thus a waste of everyone's time. Be persistent (without wasting too much time on the process), and ask for feedback if it is not given to you directly. This feedback can help you to polish the work for re-submission.

There may be a point at which persistence ceases to be a

sensible use of your time. Perhaps you have submitted a work several times, and gained only negative feedback – nobody seems to like this as much as your previous ideas! Disappointing though this is, you may need to cut your losses. Economists tend to describe this as the *sunk cost fallacy* – a tendency to persist with a flawed strategy because time, effort and money have already been invested[119]. Try not to fall into this trap. Certainly don't get rid of your problematic work altogether, but file it away and stop spending time on it for now – it may be that it can be usefully reworked at a future stage, or that a time will come further down the line when fashions change, and your potential audience will be much more receptive to this kind of work. Darwin, for example, delayed for around twenty years before publishing his ideas about natural selection[120]. However more commonly, you are simply not trying the right market. The issue of whether a piece is right for a particular audience is one of the most useful insights that you can gain from feedback on a submission. So tackle any major flaws that have been brought to your attention, and try again with a different sort of market in mind.

One strategy that can take some of the pain and hassle out of submitting your creative work is to have an agent who already has relationships with the professional markets. If that's not possible, you will need to organise this part of the process yourself, but at least make use of the (inevitable) rejections. And perhaps take a leaf out of Steven King's book – King literally hung letters of rejection on his wall to motivate him to keep working hard, improving and trying[121]. And we all know how it worked out for him.

Key tips:

- Consider each potential project that lies ahead of you, asking critical questions to assess whether it is worth the time investment involved.
- Identify a set of projects that you can give a good amount of time to, establishing a large number of plans and ideas and selecting a smaller number of projects that you are spending time on early drafts or re-working.
- Don't neglect the importance of strategy when it comes to getting your work to its final audience. Be systematic and persistent, and make perceptive use of feedback.

Conclusion

As we have seen, creativity is not really about flashes of inspiration that come only to a few, or limited to people that have a special and unique type of brain. Instead, anyone can be creative, and there are numerous steps that you or others that you work with can take. Using the strategies described throughout this book will improve your ideas and boost your creative output.

Ideas are often at the heart of innovative work, and the first few strategies have discussed how new ideas come to us. These have been explained in terms of a set of simple practices that we can put into action in order to have more, better ideas, and to make optimal use of these ideas through combinations and revisions. To some extent this process depends on a person's level of knowledge, but better and more productive creative thinking is possible at all levels and stages of expertise, from the beginner to the old hand.

As discussed in the second part of the book, though, it's not enough just to have good ideas – you also need a set of creative habits which will allow you to make the best of these. All too often, creative professionals and artists have a large stock of ideas that never come to fruition. The second set of strategies have therefore described how to develop working practices that will allow you to take projects from inception through to completion.

You can also apply the ideas in this book on a 'meta' level to your creative career itself. Creative thinking and expert knowledge, nudge strategies and motivation – all of these strategies could be applied to how you approach your field. Often, the most successful creatives are not those who have the best ideas, but the people who are best at pivoting and putting themselves in a position to be at the forefront of new technical and cultural movements. So try new things, be open minded, and always willing to learn new skills, and meet new people

Finally, it's ok to be unusual – creative fields themselves could often do with recombination of ideas and with looking at problems with fresh eyes. You don't have to follow the set path for your particular field. Indeed, doing things differently will make you a lot more interesting. Many great creative artists switched field at some point in their career. So try new things, be open minded, and always studying and learning new skills, and meeting new people. Whatever you focus on, good luck with your creative endeavours.

Index

Notes

INTRODUCTION

1 Chiltern, M. (2017, 28 February). Terry Pratchett: 50 best quotes. *The Telegraph Online.* Retrieved 20 May 2019 from https://www.tele-graph.co.uk/books/authors/terry-pratchett-best-quotes/

2   Wilson, S. (2016). Divergent thinking in the grasslands: thinking about object function in the context of a grassland survival scenario elicits more alternate uses than control scenarios. *Journal of Cognitive Psychology, 28*(5), 618-630.

3   Robinson, K. (2017). *Out of our Minds: Learning to be creative (3^{rd}Ed).*Chichester: Capstone Publishing (p. 52).

4   Harari, Y. N. (2016). *Homo deus: A brief history of tomorrow.* London: Harvill Secker.

STRATEGY 1: GENERATING IDEAS

5 Valentish, J. (2019). Interview with Ayishat Akanbi.   *The Guardian Online.* Retrieved 26 May 2019 from https://www.theguardian.com/-culture/2019/feb/26/ayishat-akanbi-my-problematic-ideas-are-my-favourite-ones

6   Guilford, J. P. (1950). Creativity. *American Psychologist, 5,* 444−454.

7   Parnes, S. J., & Meadow, A. (1959). Effects of "brainstorming" instructions on creative problem solving by trained and untrained subjects. *Journal of Educational Psychology, 50*(4), 171-176.

8   Deuja, A., Kohn, N. W., Paulus, P. B., & Korde, R. M. (2014). Taking a broad perspective before brainstorming. *Group Dynamics: Theory, Research, and Practice , 18*(3), 222−236.

9   Kris, A. O. (1997). *Free association: Methods and process.* London: Routledge.

10 Singleton, J., & Luckhurst, M. (2000).   *The Creative Writing Handbook.* Basingstoke, Hampshire: Palgrave.

STRATEGY 2: DEVELOPING EXPERT SKILL

11 cited by Yeo, L. (2017). Every minute of creativity you consume takes a life-time of experience to produce. *Medium.com*. https://medium.com/personal-growth/every-minute-of-creativity-you-consume-takes-a-lifetime-of-experience-to-produce-5660ab5a8d80

12 Cobb., V. (2008). *Marie Curie: A photographic story of a life*. New York: DK Publishing.

13 Bjork, R.A. (1999). Assessing our own competence: Heuristics and illusions. In D. Gopher & A. Koriat (Eds.), *Attention and performance XVII: Cognitive regulation of performance: Interaction of theory and application* (pp. 435–459). Cambridge, MA: MIT Press.

STRATEGY 3: LOOKING FOR CONNECTIONS

14 Gabora, L. (2017).   What creativity really is – and why schools need it. *The Conversation*. Retrieved 26 May 2019 from http://theconversa-tion.com/what-creativity-really-is-and-why-schools-need-it-81889

15 Sternberg, R. J. (1985). *Beyond IQ: A triarchic theory of human intelligence*. New York, USA: Cambridge University Press.

16 Sternberg R. J., & Lubart T.I. (1999). The concept of creativity: prospects and paradigms. In R. J. Sternberg (Ed.), *Handbook of creativity* (pp. 3-15). New York: Cambridge University Press.

17 Desmond, A., & Moore, J. R. (1992). *Darwin*. London: Penguin.

18 Anderson, M. C., Bjork, E. L., & Bjork, R. A. (2000).   Retrieval-induced forgetting: Evidence for a recall-specific mechanism. *Psychonomic Bulletin & Review*, 7(3), 522-530.

19 Klein, G. (1998). *Sources of power: How people make decisions*. Cambridge, MA: MIT Press.

20 Miyake, N., & Norman, D. A. (1979).   To ask a question, one must know enough to know what is not known. *Journal of Verbal Learning and Verbal Behavior*, 18(3), 357-364.

21 Rosch, E. & Lloyd, B. L. (1978). *Cognition and categorization.   New York*: Lawrence Erlbaum Associates.

22 Eglington, L. G., & Kang, S. H. (2017).   Interleaved Presentation Benefits Science Category Learning. *Journal of Applied Research in Memory and Cognition*, 6(4), 475-485.

23 Karpicke, J. D., & Blunt, J. R. (2011). Retrieval practice produces more learn-ing than elaborative studying with concept mapping. *Science, 331*(6018), 772-775.

24 Source: https://www.enoshop.co.uk/product/oblique-strategies?filter=Oblique%20Strategies

STRATEGY 4: FLOW, AND THE ROLE OF ATTENTION

25 Pobric, P. (2017). Why the process of painting never ends. *The Art Newspaper online.* https://www.theartnewspaper.com/interview/why-the-process-of-painting-never-ends

26 Csikszentmihalyi, M., & LeFevre, J. (1989). Optimal experience in work and leisure. *Journal of Personality and Social Psychology, 56*(5), 815-822.

27 Rhee, H., & Kim, S. (2016). Effects of breaks on regaining vitality at work: An empirical comparison of 'conventional' and 'smart phone' breaks. *Computers in Human Behavior, 57*, 160-167.

28 Baddeley, A. D. (2012). Working memory: Theories, models, and controversies. *Annual Review of Psychology, 63*, 1-29.

29 Stoet, G., O'Connor, D. B., Conner, M., and Laws, K. R. (2013). Are women better than men at multi-tasking? *BioMed Central Psychology, 1*, 18.

STRATEGY 5: DRAWING ON OTHER PEOPLE

30 Dylan, B. (2004). *Chronicles. (Vol 1).* London: Simon and Schuster. (p. 51)

31 King, S. (2002). *On writing.* New York: Simon and Schuster; Connor, A. (2013). *Two girls, one on each knee: The puzzling, playful world of the crossword.* London: Penguin Books.

32 de Kort, Y. A. W., Meijinders, A. L., Sponselee, A. A. G., & Ijsselsteijn, W.A. (2007). What's wrong with virtual trees? Restoring from stress in a mediated environment. *Journal of Environmental Psychology, 26*, 309-320.

33 Sawyer, R.K. (2007). *Group genius: The creative power of collaboration.* New York: Basic Books.

34 Amabile, T., & Kramer, S. (2011). *The progress principle: Using small wins to ignite joy, engagement, and creativity at work.* Cambridge, MA: Harvard Business Press.

35 Loehlin, J. C., McCrae, R. R., Costa Jr, P. T., & John, O. P. (1998). Heritabilities of common and measure-specific components of the Big Five personality factors. *Journal of Research in Personality, 32*(4), 431-453.

STRATEGY 6: CHANGING YOUR LOCATION

36 Woolf, V. (1953). *A writer's diary.* London: Harcourt.

37 Source: https://www.theguardian.com/lifeandstyle/2010/jul/24/change-your-life-walk-burkeman

38 Oppezzo, M., & Schwartz, D. L. (2014). Give your ideas some legs: The positive effect of walking on creative thinking. *Journal of Experimental Psychology: Learning, Memory, and Cognition, 40*(4), 1142-1152.

39 Sio, U. N., & Ormerod, T. C. (2009).   Does incubation enhance problem solving? A meta-analytic review. *Psychological Bulletin, 135*(1), 94-120.

40 Barnett, S. M., & Ceci, S. J. (2002).   When and where do we apply what we learn?: A taxonomy for far transfer. *Psychological Bulletin, 128*(4), 612.

STRATEGY 7: LATERAL THINKING AND THE POWER OF ANALOGY

41 de Bono, E. (1990). *Lateral thinking: creativity step by step*. New York: Harper Perennial. (p. 11)

42 Clark, J. M., & Paivio, A. (1991). Dual coding theory and education. *Educational Psychology Review, 3*(3), 149-210.

43 de Bono, E. (1990). *Lateral thinking: Creativity step by step*. New York: Harper Perennial.

44 Aitchison, J. (2012). *Words in the mind: An introduction to the mental lexicon*. New York: Wiley.

45 Salomon, G., & Perkins, D. (1988). Teaching for transfer. *Educational Leadership, 46*(1), 22-32.

STRATEGY 8: TAPPING INTO THE UNCONSCIOUS

46 Cosmides. L., & Tooby, J. (1999). Evolutionary psychology: A primer. Retrieved 23 September 2016 from http://www.cep.ucsb.edu/primer.html

47 Freud, S. (1933/1965). *New introductory lectures on psychoanalysis*. Standard Edition. New York: Norton.

48 Zajonc, R. B. (1968). Attitudinal effects of mere exposure.   *Journal of Personality and Social Psychology, 9*(2, pt 2), 1-27.

49 Landauer, T.K. (2011). Distributed learning and the size of memory: A 50-year spacing odyssey. In A.S. Benjamin (Ed.) *Successful Remembering and Successful Forgetting: A Festschrift in Honor of Robert A. Bjork* (pp. 49-70). New York: Psychology Press.

50 Chartrand, T. L., & Bargh, J. (1999). The chameleon effect: The perception-behaviour link and social interaction. *Journal of Personality and Social Psychology, 76*(6), 893-910.

51 Bargh, J. A., & Chartrand, T. L. (1999). The unbearable automaticity of being. *American Psychologist, 54*(7), 462-479.

52 Crick, F. and Mitcheson, G. (1983). The function of dream sleep. *Nature,* 304(5922), 111–4.

STRATEGY 9: TAKE A POWER NAP

53 https://news.berkeley.edu/2010/02/22/naps_boost_learning_capacity/

54 Williamson, A., & Feyer, A. (2000). Moderate sleep deprivation produces impairments in cognitive and motor performance equivalent to legally pre-scribed levels of alcohol intoxication. *Occup Environ Med,* 57(10), 649–655.

55 Durmer, J. S, & Dinges, D. F. (2005). Neurocognitive consequences of sleep deprivation. *Seminars in Neurology, 25,* 117–129.

56 Carver, R. (2000). On writing. In Carver, R., *Call if you need me: The uncollected poetry and prose (pp. 87–92).* London: Harvill Press.

57 Firth, J. (2015). *Higher and N5 Psychology: Student book.* Glasgow: Leckie & Leckie.

58 Ekirch, A. R. (2006). *At day's close: night in times past.* New York: Norton.

59 Anderson, J. R. (1984). Ethology and ecology of sleep in monkeys and apes. *Advances in the Study of Behavior, 14,* 165-229.

60 Lovato, N., & Lack, L. (2010). The effects of napping on cognitive functioning. *Progress in Brain Research, 185,* 155-166.

61 Source: http://www.worldlifestyle.com/health/get-jolt-caffeine-nap

62 Rasch, B., & Born, J. (2013). About sleep's role in memory. *Physiological Review, 93,* 681–766.

STRATEGY 10: REVISITING WORK WITH FRESH EYES

63 Fraser, L. (2011). *J. K. Rowling: The mystery of fiction.* Argyll, Scotland: Argyll Publishing. (p. 17)

64 Glenberg, A. M. (1979). Component-levels theory of the effects of spacing of repetitions on recall and recognition. *Memory & Cognition,* 7(2), 95-112.

65 Kapler, I. V., Weston, T. and Wiseheart, M. (2015). Spacing in a simulated undergraduate classroom: Long-term benefits for factual and higher-level learning. *Learning and Instruction, 36,* 38-45.

BONUS STRATEGY: SETTING LIMITS AND CONSTRAINTS

66 Spence, A. (2000). *Seasons of the heart.* Edinburgh: Canongate Books.

67 Editors of Encyclopaedia Britannica (2019). George Perec: French writer. *En-cyclopaedia Britannica Online.* Retrieved 18 April 2019 from https://www.bri-tannica.com/biography/Georges-Perec

68 Newell, A., & Simon, H. A. (1972). *Human problem solving.* Englewood Cliffs, NJ: Prentice-Hall.

69 Source: https://irishstudies.nd.edu/news/professor-discusses-northern-irish-poetry-and-conflict/

STRATEGY 11: GETTING GOING AND STAYING ON TASK

70 Forster, E. M. (1908). *A room with a view.* London: Edward Arnold.

71 Dweck, C.S. (2006). *Mindset: How you can fulfil your potential.*London: Robinson Books.

72 missing note tensing muscles makes you more determined – study (BPS digest)

STRATEGY 12: THE POWER OF A NUDGE

73 Milton, J. (1667). *Paradise lost.* London: Samuel Simmons.

74 Halpern, D. (2015). *Inside the nudge unit.* London: Penguin.

STRATEGY 13: NAILING DOWN GOOD HABITS

75 Source: Sher, G. (1999). *One continuous mistake: Four noble truths for writers.* London: Penguin Arkana.

76 Lally, P., Wardle, J., & Gardner, B. (2011). Experiences of habit formation: a qualitative study. *Psychology, health & medicine, 16*(4), 484-489.

77 Asch, S. E. (1955). Opinions and social pressure. *Scientific American, 193,* 31-35.

78 Haslam, S. A., Reicher, S. D., & Platow, M. J. (2010). *The new psychology of leadership: Identity, influence and power.* London: Routledge.

79 Rubin, G. (2019). The four tendencies.   *Gretchen Rubin Website.* Retrieved 4 April 2019 from https://gretchenrubin.com/books/the-four-tendencies/intro/

80 Dobelli, R. (2013). *The art of thinking clearly: Better thinking, better decisions.* London: Sceptre Books.

81 Appel, H., Gerlach, A. L., & Crusius, J. (2016).   The interplay between Facebook use, social comparison, envy, and depression. *Current Opinion in Psychology, 9,* 44-49.

STRATEGY 14: FIND THE BEST TIMES OF DAY

82 Pink, D. (2018). *When: The scientific secrets of perfect timing.*   Edinburgh: Canongate. (p. 4)

83 Currey, M. (2013). Daily rituals: Is waking up early the secret to artistic success?*Slate.com.*   Retrieved 4 April 2019 from https://slate.com/cul-

ture/2013/04/daily-rituals-is-waking-up-early-the-secret-to-artistic-success.html

84 Phillips, M. L. (2009). Circadian rhythms: Of owls, larks and alarm clocks. *Nature, 458*(7235), 142-144.

85 Pink, D. (2018). *When: The scientific secrets of perfect timing.*   Edinburgh: Canongate Books.

86 Statland, B. E., & Demas, T. J. (1980). Serum caffeine half-lives: Healthy subjects vs. patients having alcoholic hepatic disease. *American Journal of Clinical Pathology, 73*(3), 390-3.

STRATEGY 15: PLANS AND SNOWFLAKES

87 Funk, M. (2016). Joyce Carol Oates interviewed by Mia Funk.   *Creative-Process.info.*   Retrieved 20 May 2019 from https://www.creativepro-cess.info/interview-entry/2016/6/1/joyce-carol-oates

88 Yorke, J. (2014). Into the woods: How stories work and why we tell them. London: Penguin.

89 Tversky, A., & Kahneman, D. (1974). Judgment under uncertainty: Heuris-tics and biases. *Science, 185*(4157), 1124–1131.

90 Buehler, R., Griffin, D., and Ross, M. (1994).   Exploring the "planning fallacy": Why people underestimate their task completion times. *Journal of Personality and Social Psychology, 67*, 366-381.

STRATEGY 16: FROM DRAFT TO FINISHED PRODUCT

91 Slater, N. (1996). *30-minute suppers (Penguin 60s).* London: Penguin Books. (p. 40)

92 Konrad, U. (2006). Compositional method.   In C. Eisen & S. P. Keefe,*The Cambridge Mozart encyclopedia.* Cambridge: Cambridge University Press.

93 Glass, I. (2009). Ira Glass on storytelling. *This American Life.* Retrieved 14 March 2019 from https://www.youtube.com/watch?v=X2wLP0izeJE

94 Ericsson, K. A., Prietula, M. J., & Cokely, E. T. (2007).   The making of an expert. *Harvard Business Review, 85*(7/8), 114-21.

95 Hart, D. (2016).   A million words. *dorianhart.com.* Retrieved 5 April 2019 from https://dorianhart.com/2016/02/02/a-million-words/

96 Robinson, K. (2017). *Out of our minds: Learning to be creative* (3rd Ed). Chichester: Capstone Publishing.

97 Peck, M. S. (2002). *The road less traveled: A new psychology of love, traditional values, and spiritual growth.* New York: Simon and Schuster.

STRATEGY 17: RECYCLING AND RECOMBINING

98 Designboom (2015). Interview with artist Kumi Yamashita. *Designboom*. Retrieved 26 May 2019 from https://www.designboom.com/art/kumi-yamashita-interview-03-05-2015/

99 Kim, Y. J., and Zhong, C. (2017). Ideas rise from chaos: information structure and creativity. *Organizational Behavior and Human Decision Processes, 138*, 15–27.

100 Ghosh, V. E., & Gilboa, A. (2014). What is a memory schema? A historical perspective on current neuroscience literature. Neuropsychologia, 53, 104-114.

101 Truby, J. (2008). *The anatomy of story: 22 steps to becoming a master storyteller.* New York: Farrar, Straus & Giroux.

STRATEGY 18: PRESSURE YOURSELF – BUT NOT TOO MUCH

102 Hans Selye Quotes. (n.d.). BrainyQuote.com. Retrieved May 28, 2019, from BrainyQuote.com Web site: https://www.brainyquote.com/quotes/hans_selye_113009

103 Cohen, F., Tyrrell, D. A. J., & Smith, A. P. (1991). Psychological stress and susceptibility to the common cold. *New England Journal of Medicine, 325*, 606-612.

104 Yerkes, R. M., & Dodson, J. D. (1908). The relation of strength of stimulus to rapidity of habitformation. *Journal of Comparative Neurology, 18*(5), 459-482.

105 Adams, D. (2002). *The Hitchhiker's Guide to the Galaxy: The trilogy of four.* London: Picador.

106 Avey, J. B., Luthans, F., & Jensen, S. M. (2009). Psychological capital: A positive resource for combating employee stress and turnover. *Human Resource Management, 48*(5), 677-693.

107 Source: https://www.quora.com/How-many-NaNoWriMo-novels-actually-get-completed-each-year

108 Selye H. (1974). *Stress without distress.* Philadelphia, PA: J.B. Lippincott Co.

109 DeLongis, A., Coyne, J. C., Dakof, G., Folkman, S., & Lazarus, R. S. (1982). The impact of daily hassles, uplifts and major life events to health status. *Health Psychology, 1*(2), 119-136.

STRATEGY 19: THE LONG HAUL

110 Cleary, T. (trans., 1992). *I Ching: The book of change.* Boston, MA: Shambhala Publications.

111 Doidge, N. (2007). *The brain that changes itself.* New York: Viking.

112 Wilson, K., & Korn, J. H. (2007). Attention during lectures: Beyond ten minutes. *Teaching of Psychology, 34*(2), 85-89.

113 Risko, E. F., Anderson, N., Sarwal, A., Engelhardt, M., & Kingstone, A. (2012). Everyday attention: variation in mind wandering and memory in a lecture. *Applied Cognitive Psychology, 26*(2), 234-242.

114 Baird, B., Smallwood, J., Mrazek, M. D., Kam, J. W., Franklin, M. S., & Schooler, J. W. (2012). Inspired by distraction mind wandering facilitates creative incubation. *Psychological Science*, 23(10), 1117–1122.

115 Storm, B. C., Bjork, E. L., & Bjork, R. A. (2008). Accelerated relearning after retrieval-induced forgetting: The benefit of being forgotten. *Journal of Experimental Psychology: Learning, Memory, and Cognition, 34*(1), 230-236.

116 Cirillo, F. (2018). *The pomodoro technique: The acclaimed time-management system that has transformed how we work.* New York: Currency Publications.

STRATEGY 20: THE DRIVE TO FINALISE

117 Poetry Archive (n. d.) Simon Armitage interview. *Poetry Archive website.* Retrieved 1 May 2019 from https://www.poetryarchive.org/interview/simon-armitage-interview

118 Baer, J. (1998). The case for domain specificity of creativity. *Creativity Research Journal*, *11*(2), 173-177.

119 Tan, H. T., & Yates, J. F. (1995). Sunk cost effects: The influences of instruction and future return estimates. *Organizational Behavior and Human Decision Processes*, *63*(3), 311-319.

120 Richards, R. J. (1983). Why Darwin delayed, or interesting problems and models in the history of science. *Journal of the History of the Behavioral Sciences*, *19*(1), 45-53.

121 King, S. (2002). *On writing.* New York: Simon and Schuster.

About the Author

Jonathan Firth is an author, researcher, psychology teacher and teacher trainer. He writes books and resources for both students and teachers, including psychology textbooks for high school level. His most recent publications include *The Teacher's Guide to Research* (2019, published by Routledge), and *How to Learn* (2018, published by Arboretum Books).

Jonathan has been a teacher for over 20 years. Having spent many years working at high school level, he now teaches at the University of Strathclyde, Glasgow, Scotland. His research focuses on memory, learning, and metacognition.

Follow Jonathan on Twitter: @JW_Firth

and you can find out more about his latest publications by visiting:

www.jonathanfirth.co.uk/books

By the same author:

It's time to stop using flawed, outdated study techniques and develop a set of science-based study approaches instead.

How to Learn includes practical solutions for use when learning any subject. This is the guide that you need to take information in effectively, get better results, and ensure that learning lasts.

Printed in Great Britain
by Amazon